NOT DYING

Also by
WILLIAM SAROYAN

•

Boys & Girls Together

•

Here Comes, There Goes, You Know Who

•

The William Saroyan Reader

WILLIAM SAROYAN

NOT DYING

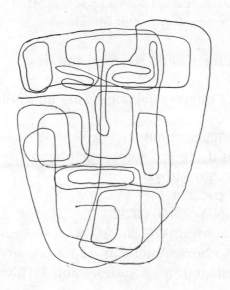

With drawings by the author

BARRICADE BOOKS, INC., NEW YORK

Published by Barricade Books Inc.
150 Fifth Avenue
New York, NY 10011

Printed in the United States of America.

Library of Congress Cataloging-in-Publication Data

Saroyan, William, 1908–
        Not dying: an autobiographical interlude / by
        William Saroyan.
            p.   cm.
        ISBN: 1-56980-081-2
        1. Saroyan, William, 1908-   —Authorship,
        2. Authors, American—20th century
        —Biography. 3. Authorship. I. Title.

        PS3537.A826Z469   1996
        818' .5209—dc20
        [8]   96-26736
                                                CIP

First trade paperback printing

To the psychiatrist in the sky

Take it as it comes—
soon enough the past, the present,
and the future will be the time it is.

INTRODUCTION

In my father's Malibu house during the summer of 1958, when I was fourteen and he was forty-nine, I first came across a book by Jack Kerouac, *The Subterraneans* in its original Grove Press trade paperback edition. Pop also had the first issues of the *Evergreen Review* which celebrated the Beat Generation and a recording of Lawrence Ferlinghetti and Kenneth Rexroth reading their poetry to jazz.

"Now, let me say this about Kerouac's book," he said when he saw that I'd begun to read *The Subterraneans*. "It tells a truth, but it's only *one* truth. It's not the only truth."

He pretty much left it at that, for he, too, a cautionary word to his teenage son aside, was interested in what the Beats had done, and especially in Kerouac, who was the sort of American literary movie-star the likes of which hadn't been seen since—well, since William Saroyan himself.

Late in his life, which ended in May of 1981 when he was seventy-two, my father asked me what had happened to Kerouac.

"He died," I said. "He drank himself to death."

We were walking in his neighborhood in the Sunset District in San Francisco, and he characteristically stopped for a moment and shook his head.

"My God," he said, "these people must take themselves awfully seriously."

It is almost fifteen years now since my father's death, and I've recently been looking through some papers of his found by my mother in storage, papers dating back to his earliest efforts and to the days of his greatest success, the 1930s and the early 1940s. The story those papers tell is phenomenal. In the middle of the Great Depression, a young man from an impoverished Armenian immigrant family took the literary world by storm, first by remaking the short story so that it seemed to be written directly to the reader by a wonderful friend, and then branching out to the Broadway theater. In a celebrated series of plays that included *The Time of Your Life, My Heart's in the Highlands,* and *Hello Out There,* he broke the hold of the traditional play form as purveyed by such practiced hands as Moss Hart, George S. Kaufman, Sidney Kingsley, and Robert Sherwood and brought a poetic, improvisatory, jazzlike enchantment to the stage, easing the way for everyone from Tennessee Williams to Eugene Ionesco.

In both his prose and his plays, he effectively took literary high-modernism and put it into a form palatable to the general public. Among his voluminous fan mail, the following letter of October 1942 from Jack Kerouac's boyhood friend Sebastian Sampas, who was killed at Anzio, is indicative of the affectionate fervor Saroyan aroused in his fans:

2 Stevens St.
Lowell, Mass.

My dear Mr. Saroyan,

This is a letter I was never going to write but somehow brooding here in the middle of the night I find myself perplexed by many things. Also I find that there are so many things I must tell you. You see October's here. I just left college. I'm 1-A in the Draft . . . My friends are gone. But let me tell you about my friends, Bill, because it was enthusiasm for your works and your ideals that bound us in comradeship.

Three years ago Billy Chandler, a friend of mine, came up to my house and asked me to read "The Daring Young Man on the Flying Trapeze"—and I remember it—

"Horizontal awakening. . . ."

(Oh! That's not quoted correctly but you get the point)

That night Billy Chandler & Jack Kerouac, another young man nurtured in the Saroyan humanism, and I went to see the sunrise. We stayed up all night, Bill, discussing our ideals, life, & all humane matters—

Jack Kerouac, Billy Chandler & I had a wonderful summer back in '39. O! I'm not saying what I want to say. I can't project the enthusiasm, the fire, the burning zeal for Truth. Anyhow Billy joined the U.S. Army that summer and was shipped to the Philippines. Where is Billy now? Jackie went to Columbia, & I continue my own schooling—

Bill, do you see what I'm driving at! It isn't my fault that I wake up in the night with half-a-million broken dreams!

Well, we read all your plays & all your stories and we were enteared [sic] with happiness the next summer when you made that statement regarding Thomas Wolfe—

Last spring Jack joined the Merchant Marines & after one trip he went back to Columbia. He is playing football there—I have reams and reams of letters Jackie sent me & one short story in which he meets Billy Saroyan—that kid really is a great writer.

Anyhow we have followed your career very closely and admire you very much. It's so hard to make this statement. I guess it's the American tradition of frowning on emotions.

I went down to see Jack 3 weeks ago & caught your play "Hello Out There" & we got tight along with 2 females & we went down to the Village exhorting mankind to seek Truth with the words "Hello Out There."

Later, that week, while Jack & I were discussing, well here's what Jack said—

"I wish we could talk to Billy Saroyan & tell him how much he means to us." But there was such a sad look on his face when he said that, Bill—

God! if only you could read his manuscripts to see the stuff he has got. Look, my main reason for writing this letter was just to tell you all this—Tell you how we were moved to tears when your plays folded on Broadway & how awful you must have felt because we both knew it was a defeat hard for you to take—

Do me this favor, Bill. It means a lot. Drop a postal card or a letter (I know how pressed you are for time) to John Kerouac, 209 Livingston Hall, Columbia University, New York City—and write a few lines—anything—It would mean so much to him. I'll finish this letter with one of Jack's paragraphs.

"If tears alone shall wash away the cruelty of the years, and nourish the white flower that grows in our black & broken hearts and teach us that life is not long & foolish, but brief & lovely, if tears alone must serve then let it be with tears."

Fraternally yours,
Sebastian Sampas

From 1934, when his first book, *The Daring Young Man on the Flying Trapeze and Other Stories,* was published to 1943 when *The Human Comedy* appeared—first as a popular MGM movie starring Mickey Rooney (for which Pop picked up an Academy Award for the best Original Screen Story) and then as a novel, a Book-of-the-Month Club Main Selection with an advance order of 350,000 copies—there was no better-known writer in America. At the same time, he was a Pulitzer Prize winning playwright who had the respect of the literary establishment.

In 1934, the young man was twenty-six years old, handsome and single, with energy to burn. In 1943, he was thirty-five, recently inducted into the army and just married to the eighteen-year-old New York debutante Carol Marcus and soon to be a father. From here on, he would never know again the kind of mythic fame he had lived with for a decade, just as Kerouac would be almost a forgotten man by his death at forty-seven in 1969, only a dozen years after *On the Road* had rocketed him to fame.

Not Dying was written during the summer of 1959 in Paris, where Pop had rented a three-bedroom apartment on Avenue Victor Hugo on the Right Bank, so that he and my sister Lucy and I could all spend the summer together. Pop was long divorced from my mother (who would remarry that summer in New

York), a single man who seemed disinclined to enter on another relationship. No longer the lean figure of his youth, he wore an old-country handlebar mustache of the kind once worn by his father, Armenak Saroyan, who had bought the family to America from Armenia and then had died at thirty-seven of appendicitis, a disappointed preacher and poet who had been unable to find his footing in the New World. At three, my father was the youngest of the four Saroyan children who, as a consequence of their father's death, had to be placed in the Fred Finch Orphanage in Oakland for the next five years.

I found that Paris summer tough going. I couldn't speak French, didn't have any friends, and had a hard time finding enough to do. I was thrown back on my own resources and spent time reading, walking, going to the track by myself now and then, and to movies on the Champs Elysees, where *The 400 Blows* had just opened. Each morning Lucy and I were aware Pop would be up at his typewriter in the front room, working on a new book.

One afternoon when no one else was in the apartment, I came across a note he had written down in hand on a piece of typing paper: "The only one I have ever really loved is Saroyan, and all that I really love now is the little of Saroyan still left in me."

It was a sad thing to read, but of course I wasn't moved to the sympathy for the bleak candor of such a note that I feel today. Most writers never have to deal with the kind of public apotheosis my father knew at his height. As the newly discovered papers attest, it had to have been dizzying. There were, for instance, three plays written by others during this period in which a character based on Saroyan is the central protagonist: *Jason, The White-Haired Boy,* and *The Five Alarm Waltz.* In the last of these, the Saroyan figure was played by the young Elia Kazan.

That summer in Paris, Pop was also working on assignment for Darryl Zanuck on a new play with a role in it for the producer's lady friend Juliet Greco. Zanuck was living at a hotel, and

Pop went to a number of meetings with him, his only business outings. As he writes, we discovered on the Left Bank the street called Rue des Beaux Arts, where for a small price one could commission an electric Tinguely sculpture to make a drawing, and we made regular jaunts there. Socially little went on with the exception of one evening when we all went to a party at the invitation of Betsy Blair, who had played the lead in Pop's play *The Beautiful People* years before. Among the other guests at this lively occasion was the director Jules Dassin, who had a beautiful daughter around my age.

Today I wonder whether during that summer my father instinctively hadn't *allowed* us to be a little bored, for that situation yielded an unexpected dividend for me. Before our arrival, Pop had met the Russian emigré painter Serge Poliakoff at a party, and he had a small book of reproductions of his work on the living-room coffee table. I immediately opened it and began exclaiming at what I took to be the simplemindedness of the paintings. They were abstractions of richly painted, solid-color, puzzlelike forms and seemed to me pointless.

I would remark on this virtually every time I opened the little book, which remained on the living room table throughout the summer. After an initial shrug, Pop remained uncharacteristically quiet and noncommittal when I made my regular denunciation. Then, toward the end of the summer, something happened. Having opened the book again and again, something in the work began to engage me. The puzzlelike forms now communicated an inner equilibrium, a visual serenity that satisfied me deeply.

This was a benchmark aesthetic experience for me, a recognition that abstract art could be as direct and powerful as any other kind of art, and it happened, I don't doubt, because my father chose not to argue or in any way mediate my experience of the work. Whether he himself got anything so rewarding from the Poliakoff works, I don't know, but he *had* gotten it somewhere, from some art, and knew it had nothing to do with being persuaded.

When *Not Dying* was published several years later, I was now a young man with nascent literary aspirations of my own, and I gave Pop a hard time for misrepresenting the summer and my part in it, by making me a "prop" of his literary creation rather than truthfully reckoning the grim interlude it had been. He was in New York at the time, having taken a penthouse apartment on Third Avenue, one he would give up almost immediately since it proved to be very noisy with rooftop fans and blowers that came with the view. He endured my assault on his work with quiet good humor, making us cups of instant coffee to which he would add the canned dehydrated milk he favored over cream.

A few years later, when my poet friend Ted Berrigan referred to *Not Dying* with admiration, it caught me by surprise. It wasn't after all the young Saroyan most people harked back to, but the less-celebrated mature writer long after his glory days.

That summer, it is clear to me at fifty-two, my father was intuitively delving into the new phase of life that men encounter at or around the of fifty. The book begins with his older brother Henry's question in a dream, *What have you done? Died?*—and the rest of it might be regarded as a wide-ranging journal on the specific nature of the change the writer finds it impossible not to notice. Here is the man himself, minus a pardonable commercial for the legend every now and then, in the process of coming to terms with this new epoch of his life. If there is a single book that signals his breakthrough into the literary terrain that would comprise the rich final phase of his career, in which he made something new of the memoir much as he had done earlier with both the short story and the play, this is it. *Not Dying* indeed.

—Aram Saroyan

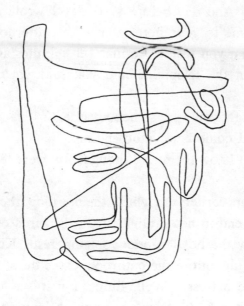

"And now, Mr. S.," the Interviewer said, "to what do you attribute your old age?"

"Not dying. Is this interview for the *Paris Review?*"

"No, this is for a paper in Dublin."

"In that case, do I have your name right? Alakhalkhala?"

"Why Alakhalkhala?"

"A favorite name."

"No, my name is Dominic Hanafin. I'm thirty-three years old, a year and a half out of Dublin. I sent you a letter a week ago, along with a written interview of fifty questions. And day before yesterday I wrote and said I would come to your hotel at two this afternoon on the chance that you would see me. Ten minutes ago I spoke to you on the telephone and you said you'd be right down."

"I thought you were somebody else."

"Shall I come back another time?"

"I don't know the man I thought you were, either."

Six hours earlier, at eight in the morning, the night had begun to end in hot sunlight, with the birds of the trees just below the hotel window singing Jesus King Christ. And, singing, out of the bathroom came the slim body of the movie actress. (Well, didn't I first see her in the movies when I was twenty?) A week later at a play at the Gymnase a young girl in a fancy house was instructed by an old girl to flatter her admirers by making a throaty noise, and the girl, misunderstanding a little, made the noise twice in a casual conversation, reminding him of the actress. Hell, he thought, it's an old trick, possibly out of the frozen North somewhere, a trick of the Eskimo girls, most likely.

Shall I write and ask her? Remember the throaty noises? What were they *for?* Togetherness? Being present? Not absent? Well, the night we met I had had five weeks of fighting off absence, which means becoming suddenly, unaccountably *out,* or nowhere.

In the stupid city of Cannes I nearly died in my sleep.

4

My brother came there and smiled, as he'd smiled in the photograph taken (somewhere in California when he'd been six and I'd been three, his arm around my shoulder) by one of those traveling photographers of 1911, for which my mother, suddenly a widow, paid him a quarter. We had sat down on a broken sofa that had been moved out of the house and placed under a China-ball tree in the weedy yard. It must have been in the town of Campbell, just outside of San Jose, where my father had just died. His dog, a white spitz with flashing eyes, stood directly in front of us, watching and waiting for any false move. Ready? And it was done. Forty-eight years ago. The Poet and his Brother. The Poet had his usual cold. His mouth was open because he couldn't draw air through his nostrils. His lips were dry, and there were two teeth marks in the middle of the lower lip. It was the Poet's eyes, though, that the traveling photographer had caught at the right moment. Wide open, fascinated, astonished, disbelieving.

Into the sleep of death and Europe my brother came, but why was he smiling that way? Hadn't I read in the *Scientific American* about a father in San Francisco who had suddenly stepped into a hotel room in New York to be with his son? They had said a few things to one another, and then the father had gone back to San Francisco, to his dead body there.

My brother said, "What have you done? Died?"

Me? What are you talking about?

But by then I was fighting for another chance.

My brother had said *died,* he hadn't said anything just a little less than that, and you know how sleep is, how time in sleep is. Did I actually come home to my room at the Majestic Hotel in Cannes, across from the Municipal Casino, at five in the morning, and did I go to bed, to sleep, and did I suddenly die in my sleep? Am I, then, dead, and know it, or is there time? Do I have an instant of time from before death, or from during it, or even from a little after it, in which to grab back my little portion? Which of us understands life? Which of us knows how death comes?

I woke up, not glad, not even alive, not even awake. But whatever it was, it was at least *something.* I was scared, because the sleep might very well have been *the announcement* of the real thing, soon to come. I got out of bed. In ten minutes, in two minutes, in one minute, in no time at all, death was gone. Again, death was gone. Had I better rejoice, or forget it? I forgot it.

"Where were we?"

"I was asking if I ought to come back another time when you fell silent."

"No, now is as good a time as any. Ask a question."

CHAPTER TWO

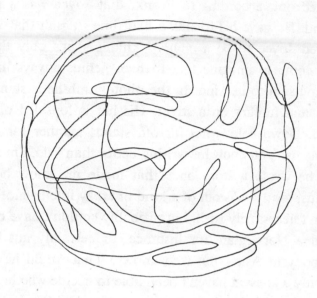

"Well, first, who do you write for? I mean, I have noticed that since the end of the war in 1945, nobody is *really* interested in reading any more, so who do you write *for?*"

"Well, you know, I can answer that question. I can answer any question you can ask, but I wonder if I should."

"All right. Who did James Joyce write for?"

"I never knew him, but there is a photograph of him at the American Cultural Center at 32 Rue du Dragon that is good to see. Frank O'Connor reviewed the memoir of Joyce written by Joyce's brother Stanislaus, and it turned out, according to Frank, that Joyce was a poor friend. He gave his friends a bad time. It isn't that I expected Joyce to be a man of kindness, it's only that I had come to imagine that men of genius always had a compulsion to be kind. In the photograph he is standing lean and hungry on a street. His hat is lopsided on his head. Down below, not far off, stands another James— Stephens. You know his writing better than I do, I'm sure, but he wrote a story once that made me know he's a genius, too: it was out of a kind of crazy intelligence that wasn't necessarily Irish, but probably couldn't have come from a Norwegian, for instance, or certainly not from anybody in Asia—but who knows? That would have to be only a guess. I haven't been able to decide whether the waiters at this hotel don't come to your table when you sit down because they believe it isn't elegant, or because they believe Americans have got to be kept waiting. What will you have, in case a waiter comes over?"

"Well, a coffee, then."

"Have some melon, first. They're from Spain, the first melons of the year, and not very good yet, but certainly better than nothing. I'll have the same—melon and coffee, and of course cigarettes. I notice you're smoking Gitanes. When I first came to Europe in 1935 it was a great pleasure to buy the cigarettes of each country I reached, and to taste the difference. Best of all were the cigarettes of Russia, about an inch of dry tobacco—the only pure tobacco in any cigarette in the world, they said—and an inch and a half of white cardboard with a little cotton in there. You could tilt the cigarette up in your teeth. The difference in the lungs of the smoke of the different nations of the world pleased me. I really enjoyed noticing it, and the smoke itself put a kind of rejoicing in my spirit. I have this inclination to rejoice, but in those days I had it bad. Cigarettes don't do it any more, though, not even my own brand, Chesterfields, which cost half a dollar a pack in Paris. So I tried Gitanes a month ago, but only three of them nearly killed me. What I mean is, you learn to live with your own poisons. You can't make it with anybody else's. And it happens that after having quit smoking for longer than half a year I took it up again suddenly in Trieste six weeks ago. And I may say I am glad I did. I saw no reason to deny myself the little leap of the spirit I get from every cigarette I smoke, especially the first one after coffee. That cigarette, whether it's in the morning or later, that first cigarette after sleep, brings me straight back to my life. To my fight with death, I mean. The theory has been for a number of years that you get cancer of the lungs from smoking, although they may have it backwards—you *may* tend to get cancer from the thing that makes you want to smoke so much, not from the smoking itself. I'm mumbling, you understand, because I'm still drunk from last night, even after brushing the teeth, shaving, showering, and putting on fresh clothes: the old ritual, that is, of coming to life. So far you're not writing anything down. Can you remember any of this, or don't you want to?"

"I can remember some of it. And of course I mean to do so, even though I'm here only because you imagined I was somebody else. Didn't you read my written questions?"

"I'm afraid not. I don't even remember *glancing* at a hundred and fifty questions."

"Fifty."

"It comes to the same thing. Waiter, at least pour water, will you? He saw us, didn't he? He looked in this direction, didn't he? He heard me, didn't he? We've only been ten minutes, I suppose, but ten minutes is a long time sometimes, and as recently as two years ago I would have gotten up and fetched my own water, and my own coffee, too, but not these days. What's the use getting annoyed with waiters? It might give you the mumps. I knew a guy in the Army who wanted to know one day if I had ever read a short story by Pirandello called *The Man with the Flower on His Tongue*, and I hadn't. Well, here's the water, at any rate. Waiter, two melons and two coffees, please. He was a major, by direct commission, a director of films who picked up British girls in little pubs and brought them to his room, where he and I and a writer and a cameraman were billeted, if you'll pardon the expression, and he closed the door of his little room, about twice the size of a closet, and all night banged away—you may know the song. He said, 'The Flower is cancer.'

"This story by Pirandello was the only thing of its kind the Major ever made a point of bringing up in a conversation. I wanted to read the story as soon as possible, but so far I haven't. I just haven't gone looking for it, and I haven't come upon it by chance, which I suppose I have imagined I would do sooner or later. I'll read it some day. The point is that he got through the war all right, he didn't do anything heroic, he didn't disgrace himself, he went back to work in Hollywood."

"May I interrupt?"

"O.K., but I've got an appointment in forty minutes, and I don't want to do this in two parts. Here's the melon, at last."

"It was nothing, really."

"No, go ahead."

"What's the name of the story by James Stephens?"

"I don't remember. We're all slobs. We can't remember anything. But it was this errand boy going everywhere lickety-split, sent by this theatrical agent in Dublin, and this big bosomy lady who had been in vaudeville, who was forever opening her arms to him and pressing him against her sweaty, powdered bosom. Read it, nobody was ever funnier. Three years later the Major was dead of cancer. His death made me remember him in London in 1944, the hurry he had always been in, the picked-up girls every night, but especially the story by Pirandello. That's all, so go ahead with the questions."

"Well, could we go back to who do writers write for *now?*"

"Who did they used to write for?"

"People, of course."

"Then that must be who they write for now, too, but are you sure they *ever* wrote for people? I mean, with that particular kind of particularity? A writer begins by writing for himself, most likely from not knowing *how* to write, and in order to find out how, or to find out that he can't. I have always believed, for instance, that if I can read the stuff, somebody else can read it, too. Thus, you begin by writing for yourself, and not failing in this you presume that you are writing for others, too. But if you haven't taken a wife yet, you find that you are writing for her, too, whoever she is, whoever she may turn out to be, and of course this means that you begin to write also for the kids she is going to have with you, or that you hope she is. You begin to write for your own human race, that is. You don't reject the rest of the human race although each of us *does* reject it somewhere along the line. It's easy to do, because where it matters most, it is easy to believe the rest of the human race has *got* to be rejected. It matters most in the majority, and in the majority the human race is pathetic. Well, who wants the human race to be pathetic? So you write for the mother of your kids, whom you haven't set eyes on yet, who may not be born yet, and for your kids with her, your own human race, which you are able to believe is going to be a superior race. But that isn't the end of the matter. You begin to write for the other fellow's wife and kids and their new human race, too. But there's still more, and this is the part that gets a little too annoying for comfort, even in mumbling like this. You write for God, which, I suppose,

12

is another way of saying something else. Try to remember if you can the time that comes to a very small child who is leaving sleep, which might be said to be heaven in a way, leaving it reluctantly but with that nagging inevitability of wakefulness, and then try to remember how *you* felt about what was next, about all of the stuff that was next, about the world—reality, I mean—not especially appealing, in fact sometimes altogether unappealing, everything cold and hostile. Well, what is it going to be? What's going to happen? Will the dangers be successfully staved off, as they were yesterday? Will the tigers fail to appear and devour the noble weak—that is, yourself? Will disease—a word you don't even know, a condition for which you have no word—seize you, putting an ache of fire in your bones and head, hissing in your ears, stinging in your eyes? Is something going to choke you? Will you burn your fingers on something? Will you fall? Will something fall *upon* you? Will you be cut somewhere? Will something get in your eyes? Christ, who can get out of bed? And yet what else is there to do? That's the way it is for a child, but it goes on as long as the child lives, and sometimes he lives a long time. Are you getting any of this?"

"Yes, of course."

"Would you rather we used up the rest of the time in short answers rather than the kind I've been making? A soft answer may turn away wrath, but a short one turns away meaning. Now, we know there is no real meaning for us, or *to* us, but there is always a

13

hope of it. In the end, I suppose, we get a little nearer to meaning by talking—and I mean carelessly—or by shutting up entirely. Take your choice. I leave it to you."

"I would like to ask a few short questions, but that doesn't mean I expect you to give short answers. What would you say is the mark of man upon nature?"

"The orderly making of a shambles."

"Anything else?"

"Of course, but not now. There isn't time. In the secret religion of every man the idea is to keep death at a distance by means of junk of all kinds, and this junk makes a shambles."

"What name would you care to give to the junk?"

"Things, of course, beginning with money, which seeks to reduce all things to the size of a coin or to a small slip of paper—that's what money *is,* for the poor man. For the rich man, it is not much more than arithmetic— numbers, counting. Nobody has ever understood money, or the action of it—what it does, how and why. By means of money comes the rest of the junk, and there is no point in naming every order of it. Possessions in general. That which is mine, not yours, not anybody else's. The more junk I have, the safer I am, or think I am. Death will have to find its way through the clutter to reach me, but even after it does reach me, I may be able to buy it off with some of my most treasured junk—in my case, that would be my writing, already written, or still to be written. My experience and skill as a writer. I may be able to trick death into letting me stay a little longer, in

order to demonstrate how a writer, how one writer, how
I myself, can do something that is likely to be fascinating,
or at any rate appealing, to death itself. To my own self,
I hope you understand, for death is always my own
death, it is always myself, it is not a stranger, I have
known it all my life; if it is not a friend (which of course
it really is, or can become at any moment), it is not an
enemy, either."

"Would you say death comes nearer to a man at fifty
than at, say, twenty?"

"No, but I say that only to keep the answer brief.
Death is always near, but probably never nearer than
it is at odd moments at the beginning of every man's time,
and then again after a dozen years have gone by and his
sex asserts itself strongly, since sex and death are very
close, almost together, almost the same thing."

"Well, what about life, then? Does life come nearer to
a man at fifty?"

"Ah, well, don't you see, we don't know. There is no
knowing. There is nothing in us, or even in nature for
that matter, that has anything like a pure accuracy; it is
always no more than an agreement of a man with himself,
or with others, about everything, and always when the
agreement is made a man knows it is useless, it isn't true,
it isn't accurate, he has left out too much, he has done a
lazy thing. We don't know who we are and we can't find
out. We therefore agree on something or other that's con-
venient. The believers, the ones who addict themselves to
a given order of belief, the Christians, for instance, in-

stead of one or another of the many others, agree among themselves that the only meaning is in Christ. The other believers, the ones who neither accept nor reject anything, who stay interested in *all* of it, or try to, sometimes agree, each believer with himself, or with his belief, that if in fact Christ is the only meaning, it follows that the ultimate usage of that earlier agreement is that every man, and especially this particular believer himself, is the only meaning. But he never forfeits any potential for a better or fuller agreement on *this* account. Sooner or later any sensible man must become bored with Christ, and with himself. And then he has got to pick it all up again and move along some more."

"Is the Pope, then, for instance, somebody, or something?"

"The Pope? Oh yes, you're Irish. I almost never think of him. Well, to me he's no more somebody or something than anybody else. But as matters stand with an enormous number of people alive in a grand ritual of agreement, the Pope among *them* is somebody special, something useful, and among the rest of us there has got to be this recognition of a kind of fact."

"Well, what I mean is, if the whole human race sud denly, or very gradually, even, became—well, let's say intelligent, reasonable, unafraid, would the Pope *still* be useful, as you say?"

"I don't see how. He is an actor. He performs a role many people believe he must perform in order that they may at first ward off death—sin, pain, disgrace—and after that be willing to receive death, without the loneliness and the probable violence that seem inevitable for the rest of us. If there is no longer this play, if there is no longer a *need* for it, how can there be any need for the leading actor in it?"

"That brings me to the actual theater. Why do we have it in the first place?"

"For the same reason that we have the church. We believe we need it—to ward off death, to postpone its arrival a little longer."

"Is a man's own life, then, a play?"

"No, of course not. The discontent of men with the lot of *man* impelled the formal play, the play on a stage, to be performed by men who pretend to die as if in life itself, and then go home and sleep with their wives. At the same time every day of every man's life *is* a play—provided a discontented man who knows how to write agrees to this, and *makes* a formal play of it. But here we are again in the same old shambles. Does God, does something, see every man a hero? Well, whether He does or not, the theory that this is so is always something anybody may choose to believe, or not."

"What is your choice?"

"I am a writer. I choose to believe that the life in *anything* is drama, that the *action or reality* of any living thing is drama. I could write a whole play in which all of the players would be worms, for instance."

"Why worms?"

"Only to illustrate what I mean. And why not? Men

and women would play the worms. I have twice made it a point to seek out the Flea Circus on Forty-second Street in New York in order to behold trained fleas in a silent drama of hops, leaps, luggings, and so on."

"Why did you do that?"

"To study the theater, of course. To study playwrighting. To speculate a little further about our own theater, which isn't, as a matter of fact, far removed from the theater of trained fleas. Now, of course, the theater of untrained fleas is the one that really matters, but it just isn't known to anybody excepting the specialist. But that theater is life itself, not art, and we are the creature which has invented art including religion—stuff on purpose, agreed upon, instead of haphazardly, with a larger form than we can behold in its entirety or out of which we can get a little comfort, a little peace, or a little amusement."

"In writing a play, do you have all this in mind?"

"In writing anything I have everything in mind, but my everything just *isn't* everything and can never be. It is only a very little of a very little of everything. The fellow in the song who tells his girl that she is his everything isn't necessarily luckier than I am, although he isn't by any means less lucky, either. He certainly isn't unlucky for the moment during which this misconception, this inaccuracy, this confusion, this faith, is valid."

"Faith?"

"Of course. What else? The man of God, as he is called, but not accurately, you understand, says the same

18

thing of God. *My* everything, and that's the word to keep your eye on. Nobody keeps himself out of anything, nobody says to God that He is Everything's everything. *My* everything."

"What is your everything?"

"Nothing. Because even a very little of everything is too much for me, for us, for anybody, for the whole human race. Therefore, the way not to die, the way to stay alive is to know this, since death alone is every man's everything. If you have got to have everything, if you have got to know everything, or only to *want* to know it, you have got to die, and what's the hurry?"

"Is there anybody you consider greater than anybody else, or greater even than everybody else? I mean, anybody who is more than another human being, if only a *little* more?"

"If I could believe such a thing of anybody, and I can't, I would have to say it was myself, and I know I am the same as any other man in this world. Have you got your interview? Because I have got to go now."

They got up and left the dining room, and he said, "I must ask you to permit me to sum up the whole thing in this manner: I am only hungover, and I have said nothing."

"Does anybody ever say anything?"

"Not really. Everybody talks all his life, and many write for many years, but nobody really ever says anything. It's all right, though."

CHAPTER THREE

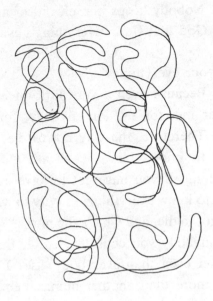

Another time, earlier, before the sleep of suffocation in Cannes, he was at the Casino in San Remo, having lost at Monte Carlo, and he said to a man he took for an Italian, not expecting to be understood, "Where do you draw the line between right and wrong?" And the man, surprising him only a little, said, "You don't. I saw you put all your chips on the red, and lose. About five hundred dollars, wasn't it?"

"About."

"You did it to win and get out of here because you're

bored. Well, a gambler can't afford to become bored. But then you're not a gambler, you're a writer. Are you bored because you have come to hate writing?"

"Yes, but perhaps only for a moment, by which I mean, you understand, a month or a year."

"Go back to your work, this is no place for a loser. Of all the cutups in the world, the Italians are the biggest. Speaking the language, being taken for one of them, I have no trouble, they try no little tricks on me, but I saw one of them shovel your win to one of his friends as if *he* had won and you had lost. You stopped the man of course, but with you he was able to make it seem a perfectly natural mistake, which it was *not,* and in the end he gave you ten thousand lire less than you had coming."

"Could be, but let the croupier's friend have it, no harm."

"That's just it. The little cutups steal your money, only in your case—not in mine—it *isn't* money, it's your way of being alive put to the test. Their stealing lets you know whatever it is you're trying to find out. What *are* you trying to find out?"

They had moved to the bar, where the bartender had automatically poured Remy Martin into a goblet, his fifth that evening; it was not yet theater-time, he could still go along to something being performed somewhere, possibly in the same building, if he felt like it.

"I am not trying to find out anything, nothing specific at any rate, although I began to gamble two weeks ago because I didn't want to go to work, but did want to have

21

all the money I need to drive a car all over Europe, and, as you know, it costs a lot of money. Not that anybody cheats us—("Ah, but they do," the other said quickly)— it's just that money being what it is, you don't want to be forever counting what you spend, or weighing the cost of something you want against the amount of money you think you can spare, and so you figure you'll get some money free of charge."

"And did you?"

"No, I reached Europe a month ago with ten thousand dollars in my pocket, and now all I have left, stashed in my room at the Royal Hotel, is fifty dollars. You seem to know my name. What's yours?"

"Hell, we met in Hollywood at a party at Stanley Rose's fifteen years ago. Or was it twenty? We were younger then, at any rate. If you don't mind my saying so, you were younger than I was, and you've changed more than I have. The fact is, you look as if you're fighting a hard fight of some kind. Jake Kosloff. Does the name mean anything at all to you?"

He saw the man back at Stanley Rose's, over the garage on Franklin Avenue, three blocks from the bookshop on Hollywood Avenue.

"Yes, the name means something to me. For instance, you were with Horace Liveright near the end of his career, and later on you went into the publishing business with somebody or other, Kosloff and somebody, I forget who."

"And I asked you that night if you had anything lying

22

around, forgotten, or half-forgotten, that you yourself liked, because if you did, I'd like to read it, and you said you had more stuff lying around than stuff in print, but you didn't like to fish through the stuff, and you had a publisher anyway. You weren't exactly rude, although the way you have makes most people hate you, if the word isn't too strong, a way of not really noticing anybody around you, not permitting them to become real to you, even, as if they were no more than figures in somebody's sleep, and not necessarily your own, as I am sure you are aware, and have always been."

"Not always, but ten years ago word came to me in a roundabout way, and, ever since, I have been at work trying to correct this unfortunate condition, but I haven't made it, I haven't corrected it, I can't excuse it, I can't find an explanation for it, I know I do nothing rude deliberately."

"I mean, here we are chatting, and I know you aren't at all interested in ever seeing me again, although if we *do* happen to meet, you won't *mind* seeing me again, and you may even be pleased about it."

"Why should I be interested in seeing you again? Except for the accidental meeting at Stanley Rose's, I don't know you. Have I got to know anybody at all? My own kids, for instance? I'm certainly not doing too well knowing myself, although I am probably making out a little better than most. All the same, if you happen to be here in fifteen minutes, I will be glad to show you how I can take fifty dollars, all the money I have in the

world, and run it up to enough for all practical purposes
—until tomorrow."

"I'll be here."

He left the bar, crossing the game room to the hall,
down the curved stairway to the main hall, out of the
building, up the street, around the Russian Church, up the
curved street to the Royal, up to his room for the last of
his money, and then straight back to the casino. He found
Jake Kosloff watching the action at a roulette wheel.

"O.K.," he said, "I say red, again."

He tossed the Italian money on the line for the red, the
marble was sent around, and it fell into the red. He let
the money lie, and it was red again.

"I've done this many times."

"I only hope you do it again, that's all," Kosloff said.
It came up red again, and he picked up the chips.

"Well, I've got four hundred dollars now, so it's time
for another brandy."

They had brandy and talked ten minutes more. Then,
he went off suddenly to a wheel in which the marble was
already rolling and he put all of his chips on the black.
The marble half walloped itself into a red, then out, then
it began to bump this way and that, and then finally it
plopped itself into the black, and Kosloff said, "What do
you do it for? Doesn't this kind of business affect your
heart?"

"Yes, it does. It gladdens my heart."

He picked up the chips and said, "Well, now I'm ahead
for the day, and so I'm getting out of here. I'm going up

24

to my room to take a shower, and then I'm going out on the town. If you've got nothing better to do, join me. I'll pick you up in the lobby of your hotel in an hour."

"Thanks. I know you mean it, but I know you'd really rather not, so I'll just loaf around some more. You *are* a fool, though, you know."

"I know, but I suppose it can't be helped. Change your mind, and let's go cat. If your wife's with you, maybe she can find a girl for me."

"My wife's here, but not with me. And that's why *I'm* gambling. I hate gambling. But get this, if you will. She doesn't want a divorce, she only wants me to stay away until she's had enough of him, and he's had enough of her, and then my wife and I are supposed to go on with our travel in Europe. And then back to Long Island, to our home, and our three daughters. And get this, too. Little by little, sick this way, mad this way, belittled this way, do you know what I'm beginning to be willing to do? To let it go, and to *have* her back. What else *can* I do? Can I do any of the things I have got to keep fighting against doing? Every minute? What has she got to give him, and what has he got to give her? She's forty-five to my fifty-five, and he's fifty-two. Is it his three-year edge of youth she wants? Is it his fat, nervous, restless body to my less fat, less nervous, less restless one? I'll be damned if I can figure it."

"Well, I'm sorry. If you change your mind, phone me at the Royal. I'll be there for the next hour."

"The life of luxury, art, and madness—is that what you said at the bar?"

"Who knows what I said at the bar?"

"Well, it *is* what you said, but *why* did you say it? To *me,* I mean. The luxury was right enough for me in a kind of general way, the art was wrong for me, but the madness came straight home. I *am* out there, you know. But I'm coming back little by little. Did you *notice* that I was out there, or what?"

"The wonder of it is that you imagine you have never been mad until now. I have always been mad."

"And *proud* of it? Is that what you mean?"

"Well, certainly not ashamed of it. Don't die—of a heart attack. Don't kill anybody, either. And good luck to all three of you."

"What right has *he* to good luck?"

"The same right as I have, the same as you have. I don't know him, I don't need to know him, I don't want to know him, I can't stand him, and yet I know he is myself, and you'd better know he's *yourself,* too. Isn't *he* dying, too? So wish him a little luck; it's the same as wishing yourself a little."

He went back to the hotel the long way, to be walking and breathing the air that had a little of the sea in it, taking the way that stayed near the sea, near lawns and flowers and bushes and trees, and he didn't mind at all that he had lost the ten thousand dollars. The eight hundred he had in his pocket wasn't the ten thousand restored, but it *was* something. He had the little red car, the little red scooter, as he called it, the German motor with the Italian body. He had driven the thing from Belgrade to Zagreb, to Trieste, to Venice, to Milan, to Domodossolo, to Geneva, to Lyons, to Aix-en-Provence, to Nice, to Monte Carlo, to San Remo. He was tired of racing the little red racer all over the place. He was tired of his place behind the wheel, and tired of the little toy itself. He wanted a good supper, he wanted a good book to read, he wanted to sleep, and the hell with the rest of it.

With the ten thousand dollars he was to have found a little house somewhere, he was to have paid cash for it, he was to have written to the boy of fifteen and the girl of thirteen, and they were to have come and to have had themselves a happy summer, so now what?

The man phoned just as he was leaving his room after a bath and three glasses of cold water out of the tap: "Can you come back to the casino? My wife is here with *him,* and I don't know what to do."

He took a taxi, to make it quick, and found the man at the bar.

"The trouble is I *can't* wish them luck—and I don't mean at gambling. I *know* they'll lose at gambling."

"Let them be. Get out of here."

"At least go and *look* at them. They're at the first roulette table. You'll know them the minute you see them."

He went out and saw them, a fleshy woman heavy with jewelry, and a fat little nervous man who seemed to have eight arms. He studied their faces a moment and knew they needed every bit of luck they could possibly get. He went back to the man at the bar and said, "Come on, let's go eat, they're just fine."

They took a taxi to a place on the water, they ate and drank, and then they began to walk back to town. Two girls, neither of them over twenty-five, loitered, waiting for them. They were pretty girls, but the husband wasn't with it, so they went back to the casino.

He put five dollars on number thirteen and it came up, so he took a place at the *chemin de fer* table. When the bank came to him he bet twenty, won, won twice again, and passed the bank. The man who bought the bank dealt his opponent a nine, himself an eight, screamed in Italian, and left the table in a rage.

At three in the morning when he said so long to Jake Kosloff he had run up the five dollars to more than five hundred and he felt that he had done right in putting writing out of his mind.

CHAPTER FOUR

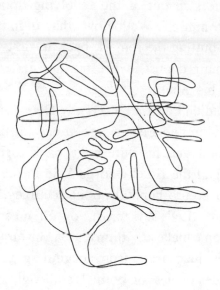

Now, in the hotel lobby in Paris, having just remembered Jake Kosloff in San Remo, and having just remarked to the Irish newspaperman, "This is how we live, and how we go to our graves—hungover, confused, and stupid," he had the feeling that Jake Kosloff was near, that he would see him soon, almost instantly.

The newspaperman said, "I want to quote you accurately, but I'm sure I can't, so if it's not too much trouble, can I bring around what I write, so you can check it for accuracy?"

While the newspaperman was speaking, he saw Jake Kosloff's wife step out of the revolving door, and then he saw Jake himself. Well, now, that didn't hurt a bit, he thought, putting the remark back in time forty years, when the young dentist in Fresno had pulled an aching tooth out of his mouth.

Oh, no, it didn't hurt a bit, Dandy Dentist, sir—it only let me know I'm dying at the age of eleven, that's all, sir.

Jake Kosloff and his wife were back together again, and stopping at the Hotel George V in Paris.

"Let's not be too hopeful about accuracy," he said to the Irishman. "Let's *try* for it, by all means, but let's know we won't make it. In any area, in any dimension. Our story is inaccurate from beginning to end—misunderstandings or lies, or both. It's all right, though, because there really isn't a lot of difference between the accurate and the inaccurate. We like to think there is, of course, and of course we should, but there isn't. Our mark —and it is not entirely without a certain kind of charm, if you follow me, if you understand that even my way of trying to put it is inaccurate—our mark, the thing that identifies us unmistakably (in relation to baboons, if you like) is nervous, feverish, hysterical stupor, and at our best a steady rage about this, a continuous awareness of it, an annoyance with it, a longing to be done with it suddenly, by some kind of magic, and forever after to be more than we are. *Try* for accuracy, and let me have a look at it. You won't make it, but you may come up with something just as good."

He noticed that Jake Kosloff had noticed him, but just as he himself had not made anything of having noticed Jake Kosloff, he was not surprised that Jake Kosloff had not made anything of having noticed him. Why should he? Why should either of them? And at the same time he suddenly recognized the man who had just gotten up out of one of the heavy chairs in the lobby and was now waiting to speak to him. He believed that this was the man he had believed the Irishman to be, the man he had never before seen, who had spoken to him twice on the telephone, and had written to him once, a newspaperman again, this time an American one, the European correspondent for a New York newspaper. That's how it is at the Hotel George V, he thought, and to the Irishman he said, "Well, I think this is the man I believed *you* were."

Jake Kosloff and his wife lingered at the porter's counter, ordering tickets for the theater, and now they turned away, to go up to their apartment.

"Well, thanks very much," the Irishman said. "I want to write this before I forget it. Will it be all right if I get back with it sometime tonight? If you're not in, I can leave it at the desk, and after you've checked it you can phone me."

"Yes, but please try to keep out a little of the pomposity. I tend to talk big when I'm hungover."

The Irishman offered his hand in farewell just as Jake Kosloff and his wife approached. They were busy chatting but Jake Kosloff saw him again, and just after the Irishman went off, and while Jake Kosloff's wife went down the hall, Jake Kosloff came up and said, "Jake Kosloff. We met in San Remo a couple of months ago, but you meet so many people I'm sure you've forgotten. I've told everybody I know how you took your last fifty dollars and ran it up to a thousand. My wife was especially impressed by your performance. Will you have dinner with us Friday night? That's day after tomorrow."

"Could you make it Tuesday?"

"We fly back to Long Island Monday."

"I'll phone you when I'm free, then, and if you and your wife are free, too, we'll take it from there."

Jake Kosloff went on, and the man who had been seated in the heavy chair in the lobby came a little closer. He carried a thin leather briefcase and two books.

"Dave Hacker," he said. "I know. You don't have to tell me. You forgot our appointment. But that's all right, because an hour in this lobby is more fun than going to the theater. Can we sit down and have a cup of coffee? I can get my story in fifteen minutes, I think."

"I had an idea I had got things balled up, and now I'm late for an appointment at the Plaza-Athénée. I'm going to walk it, though, in case you want to come along. I don't expect to hurry and it ought to take us the fifteen minutes you need. If the worst comes to the worst, we can sit down on one of the benches under a tree."

"Good enough. My paper wired me to ask about your taxes, that's all, but I may get enough to do a little piece for the *Reporter* or the *Nation*."

They went out to Avenue George V and began to walk toward the Plaza-Athénée on the Avenue Montaigne.

Fifteen minutes later they were there, and the American newspaperman said thanks and so long.

The man behind the counter at the Plaza-Athénée handed him the telephone, and Yancey said in his loud voice, "I'm coming down to the Relais, let's meet in there."

At the bar, waiting for Yancey, he answered the bartender's glance with a request in English for a Scotch on the rocks with a twist of lemon peel. Yancey came in and took a table in the corner, moving slowly for a man who was famous for a lifetime of swift movement. He ordered something in French, and then he said, "Just now, coming through the door, I remembered a dream I had last night, and then all of a sudden I forgot it, and right now I'm almost remembering it again. Now, what the hell was it I dreamed?"

Well, he thought, maybe it was something like what I dreamed in Cannes not so long ago, but he didn't say anything, thinking at the same time, Well, I guess it happens to every man after he's reached the age of fifty, as I have, or fifty-five or fifty-six, as this man has, but how should I know, there is really no telling about anybody else. It seems as if he might have had a dream of the same kind, though, from the way he spoke of it and wanted to remember but couldn't.

"Christ," Yancey said, "does it ever happen to you

that when you want to remember something you think you have *got* to remember, you just *can't?*"

"It does, but I seem to be able to remember *enough,* for all practical purposes. Maybe there's something to be said for not being able to remember. Maybe forgetting isn't so bad, either."

"Coming through the door I *had* the whole thing, and then I lost it. About a ship? Was that what it was? But I can't remember *what* it was about a ship, or even if it *was* a ship. Did you order something? The hamburgers are very good."

"I'm not eating. I eat too much. I weigh too much. I have got to get rid of the lard I'm lugging, but I've been saying that for fifteen years. I can live with it, I guess, but I still long for the time when I was a little underweight, always hungry, and burned up everything I ate, which was a lot, and not fancy, either. I'll just have another Scotch on the rocks."

"I asked you to come here," Yancey said, "because I'm flying to Cannes tonight for the film festival. I know you work swiftly, so I thought we ought to talk about the play once more before you write it. How is it going?"

"I'm off to a good start, I think, and that means the thing will be finished on schedule."

"What *is* the schedule?"

"I've given myself nine days, I've worked three, so I've got six to go. In a week, then, it'll be finished. After that, it has got to be typed, with four or five carbon copies, and I guess that'll take somebody two or three days, too. Fig-

34

ure you'll be seeing it in ten days or so. I've finished the first act. I finished it last night at a little after midnight. Two acts to go, three days for each act. It's a generous schedule."

"Is it along the lines of the story in your one-page outline?"

"Precisely, except for the stuff you know has got to come along *as you write*. You can never predict what the stuff is going to be; you work and wait for it, and watch it, and consider whether it's what you really want, and sometimes it is, and sometimes it isn't."

"But you prefer to put it into the play form, is that it?"

"Yes, because a work has got to be itself in a way that is clear and unmistakable, and a writer has got to work in a form he has worked in before. I could write what is known as a screenplay if I *had* to, if there was anything at all to be gained from it, but I don't think there is. First of all, there really is no such form. A screenplay is something like a map for a producer and a director. You don't write with words at all, actually. You don't use language, you use signs. But the play *is* being written. After it is written, you can have it *adapted* for a film. You'll get a better film that way—the best I could ever expect to write, that is—and at the same time I'll get a play. I write at least one play a year anyway, and for almost twenty years I haven't offered any of them to Broadway producers, so it won't matter if this one joins the others and isn't produced for a long time to come, long after you've shot your film and released it, and the thing has made its way, earned back the cost of production, and a profit, or flopped."

"Do you think this one is going to flop?"

"Who knows? A lot depends on how the thing turns out in the first place, and I have got to believe it is going to turn out just fine. And after that a lot depends on how you produce it—that is, on who you hire to direct it, and who you hire to play the various parts. The element of the accidental in a thing of this kind is constant. The reason I have confidence in the kind of accidents my being at work on a new play is likely to impel is that these accidents have been pretty good in the past, in all of the plays I have written. But let's face it, as the saying is, *anything* can flop. No need to be afraid of that at all. If you get a kick out of doing it, if you like doing it, if it's fun, if everybody understands that the doing of it isn't going to hurt anybody, and isn't going to solve any of the problems of the world, certainly none of the political ones, or any of the problems of people trying their best to put up with themselves and with time and change, then your chances of coming up with something halfway O.K. are improved. I get the impression that everybody puts a little too much importance into everything, with the result that ease is lost, *prohibited,* in fact, and isn't ease the thing everybody is really after?"

An hour later the meeting adjourned and he began to walk back to the George V, to his waiting work.

The problem of the play he was writing was this: to have them all the way they are anyway, to have them mistaken and mistaking, to have them earnest and near despair, to have them liars and deceivers, doubters and deniers, to have them forever troubled and nagged-at by themselves and by whoever they know, and yet at the same time to have them not unpleasant, not unattractive, not charmless, not stupid exclusively, only almost exclusively.

Later, many days after he had finished the writing of the play, long after he had revised it, long after the play had been typed, revised again, and typed again, he turned in his report to God, as he always did:

I went in there with every intention of writing something that might not annoy You for its falsity, even though it was written for money. I took after this last chance to make something that might delight You, but now that the work is finished and there isn't anything I can do about it, I am sorry that I didn't do as well as I had believed I might, fighting all the way, working with everything I had, and always praying. Even so, perhaps You will agree that what I wrote entitles me to another chance.

Forty years ago when he first began to write, he believed God turned away from the other stuff He was watching and glanced at him and said, "Who are you to think you have something to say? Who are you to think you can come into my realm and take my nature?" And he believed God might very well knock him down for the impertinence. All the same, he kept trying, and little by little God let him be. Every now and then God turned

37

away from watching all of the other stuff, most of it more important than his stuff, surely less secret than his, and God glanced at him, but soon God stopped nagging at him about who he believed he might be and about what he believed he was doing. And that was how it was when he believed he must find his woman and start his own human race. God turned and spoke again. "Who are you to reject the race I have taken ten or eleven million years to make? Who are you to think you can do better in the nine months it takes any man and woman to assemble and deliver another variation of my idea? Watch it, or I may have to give you a little surprise."

And after they had arrived, after they had each had a little of the time they were allotted, whatever the final amount of it might turn out to be, and after he and the mother had come to know them a little, he knew she and he hadn't made it, they *hadn't* started a new human race at all. They had had a couple of kids, that's all. They were good kids, as kids come, as kids go, but you just couldn't pretend they were different, or more, or better than any other kids. They were kids, and they were their own kids, whatever that meant, and since neither of them, neither the father nor the mother, had ever really found out very much about themselves, about their own fathers and mothers, all they could believe was that they had founded a family, but it didn't even remain a family for very long, and ten years ago, in 1949, he picked up and left her, although it wasn't that simple; it was more as if she had made it known to him that she wanted him to pick up and leave her, and there was no choice, although the going troubled him everywhere he went. That was when he began to know for sure that he hadn't started a new human race. He had helped put a boy and a girl, a man and a woman, among all the others in the world, at best his own, and her own, but essentially nobody's, essentially the world's own, essentially orphans.

CHAPTER FIVE

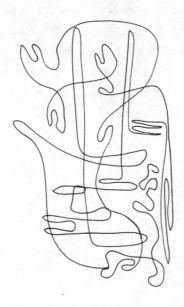

One day in Belgrade he had read in the Paris *Herald Tribune* that his Spanish publisher had been killed in an automobile crash. Two years earlier the publisher had driven him and his two kids from Barcelona to Sitges, and he had said to the publisher, "Why do you drive as if we haven't a moment to lose?" But the publisher had taken this for a compliment and had gone right on revealing his true nature through his style of driving: a swift, unstoppable, forceful, daring, brilliant, ruthless, cruel, laughing nature, full of joyous contempt for old women lugging heavy bundles, dreamy cows crossing the highway, carts drawn by weary horses, frightened drivers in old decrepit cars—all of them listening with terror to the horn, all of them turning to watch the roaring black Cadillac and to hate it and its driver—joyous contempt for people without money, without importance, joyous contempt for life, for danger, for death itself.

"Well, now, look," he said at last, "your kids aren't in this car, and mine are. Let's think of *them.*" But the publisher crashed on, saying in Spanish, "My English is not so good."

Now, as he himself drove away from Belgrade, he remembered the roly-poly swift-moving Catalonian publisher, and he thought, Hell, it could happen to anybody in a car, the way people express themselves by their driving, and I've been going along at a pretty good clip myself; slow down a little.

A few days later he slowed down a little, but picked up speed suddenly in a race with a passenger train, nearly hit a truck head-on when he shouldn't have passed three slow-moving cars blocking his race. (The driver hauled the truck off the pavement onto the dirt.) This slowed him down again, but only for a moment. He came to a swift-moving stream, the Rhone, and began to race the Rhone. He *couldn't* slow down, take it easy, believe there was no place he needed to reach in a hurry. When darkness came, though, he *had* to slow down, because he couldn't see, and so it was eleven at night when he finally reached Aix-en-Provence. He believed it was only luck that had

41

kept him from killing himself, the good luck, for instance, of having the kind of driver at the wheel of the truck who would be willing to move an enormous swift-moving heavy-laden vehicle off the highway in order not to smash a little red toy, obviously driven by a criminal. And so he felt that he had been spared. All the same, he was annoyed with himself, and with his whole absurd, lucky life.

Ten years ago, in 1949, he had taken a taxi from Marseille to Aix-en-Provence in order to visit the gambling casino, and he had won a couple of hundred dollars in five minutes. So he decided to stop in Aix, shower, change clothes, quiet down, have two drinks, a good supper, and then do a little gambling again. There was no shower, he had three drinks, skipped supper, and began to gamble as if he were offering money to God for sparing his life. "What do I care about money, after having had my life spared—again?" He drank and gambled steadily until the place closed, around four in the morning. When he added up what he had lost and learned that it came to exactly fourteen hundred dollars he thought, That's exactly the amount I paid for the car two days ago in Belgrade. He didn't mind the loss of money because he felt he had gained his life.

He was at the edge of the gambling country, and there was still plenty of time. He would mosey along into it, and he would win, because he was who he was.

At Geneva that morning he had taken the road south instead of north, because he'd been afraid to go to Paris. The Americans in Paris will be lousy with money, and who wants to see *them?* He drove in the opposite direction because he didn't want to go to work, didn't want to write, didn't want to earn money by writing. He didn't even want to try. He wanted to get money by gambling. He believed he could do it and not need to go to Paris at all. He wanted to hang around in the south, buy a small house with a small vineyard, and be there easily and thoughtfully. He needed fifty thousand dollars for the tax collector, but that wasn't much. (Joe Louis needed a million.) If necessary, he could forget the tax collector, he could become resigned to the debt, resigned to the hopelessness of ever paying it, even. What debt? Was the tax collector his father? Most of all he drove south because he didn't want to write, didn't want to think about writing, wanted to forget that he had ever written, or that he would ever write again. His typewriter had remained in its black battered case ever since it had been placed in the case at the Royalton Hotel in New York the morning he left New York and began his journey to Belgrade. He had been happy not to bring it out.

I've had it, he thought. I decided to write, and I wrote. The plays were produced, performed, and witnessed. The stories appeared in magazines, and later in books, and the novels were published and read. The money came and went, and I've had it.

For six years he had lived in a little house on the beach at Malibu, watching the shore birds on the beach, the whales moving slowly south from the north, the seals swimming silently to the shore and lying on the hot sand

43

until dogs came along and drove them back into the sea, the little lizards basking in the sun on the front porch, the gophers in the garden, the sparrow hawks that lived in the eaves of the house next door, the hummingbirds that came to the blossoms of his trees, the slow-moving skunks that came down from the hills after dark almost every night to have a look around and to leave their cool pungent smell in the fog from the sea. He had been out there with the sea, the birds, the lizards, the rodents, and the animals. At least twice a year, driving home late at night or early in the morning, he had seen a young deer at the side of Malibu Road, and he had stopped to watch it bound up the hill and disappear. Once he had seen a little red fox, and another time a slow, thoughtful mountain lion, each of them on the prowl for a stray chicken.

During the six years at Malibu, the six years of having his back turned to the world, he had worked and waited, and finally he had decided he wanted to work no more, to wait no more. And that was how it came to pass that he believed he had stopped writing the day he had left New York, had left San Francisco, Malibu, and America, and had set out for Europe, even though he had taken the typewriter along.

How much in money had he earned during the six years in Malibu? A quarter of a million dollars, most likely. And how much did he have? He had nine thousand dollars in traveler's checks and nine hundred in new one-hundred-dollar bills, or at any rate that was what he'd had when he'd left New York. He had paid fourteen hundred dollars for the red car, and he had lost the same amount at the casino in Aix. Now he was installed in a grand room at the Ruhl Hotel in Nice at eight o'clock in the evening. Soon he would go to the casino and see about his luck. He would find out if he would be able, at last, to go right on not writing for a long time, perhaps for ever.

After the age of twenty, after going to New York in 1928, after returning to San Francisco in January of 1929, after having worked at various jobs from his eighth to his twentieth year, he had never again worked steadily at any job; he had only taken a few jobs which he knew he would soon leave, or Saturday jobs, and then, soon, he had taken no jobs at all. His only source of money had become writing and gambling. He had had success in each, and failure in each.

Gambling is many things, but most of all it is a heightening of the process of waiting, and by the time he reached Nice he wanted that heightening. He wanted the instantaneous challenge, the instantaneous acceptance of it, and the instantaneous outcome. He had no fear, no anxiety, no care, no thought for the risk of any challenge, he accepted it, believing that he couldn't lose, and even at two in the morning, when he stopped to do a little arithmetic and noticed that he had lost almost three thousand dollars, he was not alarmed; he went back and played some more, and soon, around four in the morning, the cards turned and the numbers came up for him. There was a little American standing behind his place at the big *chemin de fer* game, who kept saying, "All right, now, you won that one, and you're going to win this one, too, just go right ahead, they think you're drunk and they expect you to lose the way you *have* been losing all night, but you're just not going to lose any more, because I'm right here watching." He kept the box for seven passes, betting the limit of the table, and then at last he dealt a nine to his own eight, and before the little man could tell him what to do he left the game and cashed in his chips. After the chips had been converted to bundles of French currency he said to the little man, "Now, you brought me luck, and I want to know what I can do for you. I've got all this money, and you can have as much as you need to get back into the action and win—I'll stand right behind you, just as you stood behind me." The man laughed and said, "But I've *already* won. Not anything like the amount you've won, but then I play very carefully and I don't bet very much, and I was never in trouble, I never lost, and I know you lost plenty before you began to win. You can buy me a drink, though, and I can tell you about my boy, because he wants to write, and he'll be awfully excited when I tell him I met you at the Mediterranean Club in Nice, and saw you lose a lot, and then win it all back, and a lot more besides."

They sat down, and the man told him all about himself, all about his life, a man from New Haven, the vice-president now of the insurance company he went to work for almost fifty years ago as an office boy, a man not exactly rich but certainly not in financial trouble, a widower two years, with this one son, now twenty-two.

It was a grand time in the world, because he'd bought back all his traveler's checks, and his pockets were bulging with money. The hell with writing, and the hell with *ever* going to Paris.

CHAPTER SIX

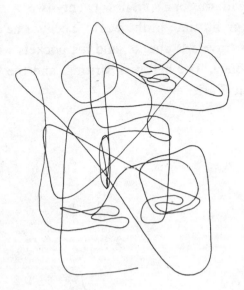

But that isn't the way it goes.

There is a Municipal Casino in Nice as well as the privately owned Mediterranean. He went to that place, too, and it was there at the membership desk that he met Vrej (which in Armenian means Revenge), who, in addition to being able to remember every new arrival at the casino, knew the real-estate situation in and around Nice, not excluding St. Tropez and Grasse.

"Last night I won almost two million francs. How much can I buy a house for?"

"That's a lot of money in France," Vrej said. "Let us go and look at a few houses before the money disappears."

They looked at three houses, but each was old and poorly located, and the price of none was lower than ten million francs, or twenty thousand dollars.

"Tomorrow," Vrej said, "let us go farther out, to where the houses are newer and have orchards and vineyards and cost less."

And so, back at the Mediterranean that night, he thought, Well, suppose I go on having the good luck of last night, and suppose I win, instead of two million, three, four, or possibly even ten? If I do that, I will buy the first likely house in the country, and there will be no *reason* to go to Paris, no reason to write stuff for money; all I will have to do is get acquainted with the house and vineyard and neighbors, and be prepared to send for my kids as soon as they are out of school. That will be a real achievement, so now as I get set for the hard work ahead, drinking brandy, let me keep this plan in mind, and play accordingly.

Dostoevsky at Baden-Baden wrote in his journal that the reason he lost was this: At the crucial moment, he lost *faith*. After which, it was *impossible* not to lose his money, too.

And a man in a restaurant was served a lobster with only one claw, so he complained to the waiter, who said, "The lobster had a fight with another lobster." The man said, "Well, why do you bring *me* the loser?"

49

After he had used up all of his French currency, after nothing had gone right, after there was no indication that he was in the proper dimension of grace to compel a change in his luck, he refused to stop, stubbornly waiting for the arrival of his true luck.

At last it *did* arrive.

He won, and then he won again, and the tide appeared to be turned, but just at that moment the big players (and winners) got up and left the game, and nobody remained at the table who was willing to risk more than ten or twenty dollars at a time.

After he had struggled with this pitiful situation until six in the morning, the game broke up, and he went home.

At ten Vrej came in his car, and they drove up into the hills and began to look at more houses.

After they had looked at three Vrej said, "Have you lost *all* of your money?"

"Almost, but tonight I'll win it all back, and tomorrow I'll pay cash for a house, and forget gambling."

He was a week in Nice, and then he decided to try his luck in the next place, Monte Carlo, so he packed his bags and loaded them into the small red racer and drove there. He didn't even take a room at the Hotel Paris, he just parked the car, and went straight to the casino.

From Monte Carlo he went to San Remo, and then he *had* to go to Paris, after all.

After three days in Paris he found out where Yancey

was staying, phoned him, and the following afternoon went there.

"This is why I'm here. I've been gambling on the Riviera a month, and now I'm broke, so I want to go to work. I want to make back what I've lost, and then I want to make enough to pay the tax collector and get him off my back."

He read the stuff Yancey owned, or was thinking of buying, and he wrote reports on the stuff, saying that most of it was no good, since that was so, and then late in April he began to write the play.

There were interruptions of all kinds, exterior and interior—interviews, lunches, dinners, social events, steady drinking, hangovers—and then back to work on the play, with everything recent and everything old becoming an element of one sort or another *in* the play, which had to be a play about change, and the humor and sorrow of it, until it was finished, and Yancey bought it for sixty thousand dollars.

When the Interviewer from Dublin came back he said, "But there are surely worse things than *not dying,* aren't there, Mr. S.?"

"Name one."

"Well, for instance, a man with a very painful incurable disease might very well find *living* worse than dying, or at any rate less attractive."

"It doesn't matter very much that anybody at any time finds living less attractive than dying, or *thinks* he does, for at best that is what it comes to: a theory. What it means is that a man is in trouble with time and himself and wants to get out of the trouble. Becoming dead is of course the final escape from one's self, the final refuge, although nobody can be absolutely sure of this because the dead stay dead. The truth may be that a man leaves one order of trouble only to find himself in another, but I would rather not talk about this, because it gets us nowhere, and we want to believe we are always getting somewhere, don't we?"

"Well, all right, if you say so. May I begin a new train of thought, so to say, by asking if you are religious?"

"Yes."

"You are religious?"

"Yes, you may ask if I am."

"Are you?"

"I don't understand what is meant by that word, I wonder if anybody does, but after we have agreed that we don't know what we are talking about, I would be willing to remark, I would in fact be compelled to remark, that I believe I prefer remaining in this world to leaving it, and that I take great pleasure in noticing that I have not left it."

"Do you feel that this belief, this preference, indicates that you *are* religious?"

"I'm not sure, but then the thing that I am *about,* the thing I have for the greater part of my life *been* about, is to consider and reconsider, and then to consider and reconsider again, in the expectation of either finding out or of *knowing* it is impossible for me to find out. I don't know. I mean, of course, that I don't know anything, with absolute certainty, with finality, with (if you like) *final* finality."

"Does this constant considering and reconsidering perhaps constitute a personal condition which might be said to be essentially religious?"

"Not if we don't know what we are talking about, as we don't. It constitutes a state of *something*, though. What do you really mean, for instance, when you ask if I am religious? Do you mean am I able, willing, or compelled to *believe*? Well, of course I am, as you are, but I do not consider that this means I am religious."

"Very well, then. What do you believe?"

"In a radio program called *This I Believe*, a man who had come along quite nicely over the years and now managed a tin factory or a chain of shoe stores or had a job as confidential secretary to somebody or other talked for three minutes along the general lines of personal belief. I found these talks fascinating in that they were invariably meaningless, and yet for all that not entirely useless—but you must understand that there is *nothing* that is *ever* entirely useless. In any case, it is impossible not to believe, and I don't mean this or that, specifically, I mean *all*, beginning (and almost ending) with the truth that one *is*, one breathes. I myself was invited about ten years ago to say in three minutes what I believe, and so, late one night—it couldn't have been ten years ago, it must have been only four or five, for I lived at Malibu at the time—I got up and turned on the tape-recorder I had in the house and I talked into the microphone for three minutes, and the next day I sent the tape to the man who had invited me to say something."

"What did you say?"

"Nothing, but the tone of voice might have meant something, especially to people in penitentiaries."

"What sort of a tone of voice was it?"

"Hushed, I suppose I might say. I had caught two or three dozen of these recitations on the radio, generally late at night, generally by accident, and I noticed that the voices were almost always morning voices, not night voices, and this seemed unfortunate. Everybody was booming along at a very swift, keyed-up pace, reading written stuff, prepared stuff, and determined not to leave out one word. After less than fifteen seconds the words became meaningless of course—that is, even more meaningless than they were in any case—and all you were able to hear was a hearty, booming voice. Something like a dreary song, although that isn't very accurate, either. What it was was jabbering, and all it did was annoy you. I imagined convicts of all kinds all over the country, and sick people in hospitals, trying to listen to the stuff, and trying to make a little sense of it. Well, it couldn't be done. A man who obviously considered himself a success was simply passing along to others, total strangers, this theory of personal success, all the while pretending that he was saying something else, something better, something about what he believed. Nobody said anything anybody could listen to for a real meaning of any kind. If you want to know how to get to sleep sometime when you can't sleep, turn on the radio to somebody talking. I think it will do the trick."

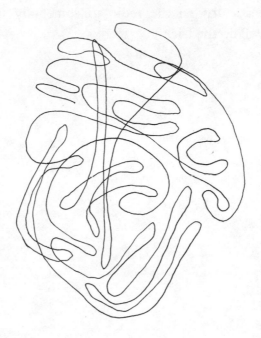

CHAPTER SEVEN

My son and daughter came from New York to spend the summer, and one afternoon I took my son in a taxi to St. Cloud, while my daughter stayed home to read.

On our way we believed we would miss the first race and possibly the second, but when we reached St. Cloud there was still time to get a small bet down on the first race, which got off forty minutes late. We bet Saxe, and the race finished Cantavale, Antilope, Quitte ou Double, La Vrille, Brasilia, *Saxe,* Rochemaure, Mon Beau Rêve, and Sissi III. Sixth, in short.

I said, "Now, I want you to have fun. It's a beautiful day, we've got a table booked at Maxim's for half past seven tonight, we've got a lot of money, we live in a fine apartment, things arc going very nicely for all of us, and I don't want you to get all worked up if your horse doesn't win."

"I didn't come out here to throw away my money."

"No, you didn't, but it may happen just the same."

"In a pig's eye. I don't know about you, Pop, but I'm going to win."

"O.K., who do you like in the second?"

Ten minutes later, after considering a lot of stuff in a paper called *Paris-Turf,* he said, "The winner is Kyrger," only he pronounced it Kryger.

Now, in the usual rush to get into the clubhouse, to get a bet down before it's too late, we had neglected to buy a program, and after wc had been at the track fifteen or twenty minutes we couldn't find anybody *selling* programs. I saw a program—it might have been yesterday's, of course—on the lawn, picked it up, and noticed that it was the program we wanted. Not only that: it had been dropped by a player who had picked a horse in every race, but in the first race his horse had been Brasilia, which had done no better than our horse Saxe, so we weren't inclined to pay very much attention to his choices.

My son bet Kyrger one thousand francs to win, and one thousand to place, and I went along with him at five thousand francs to win and five thousand to place. The horses finished El Gitanillo, Incitatus, Emissa, *Kyrger,* Don Pedro, Rebel, Le Mioche, Audacieuse III, and Mon Dernier. Our horse was fourth this time, instead of sixth. I looked at the program and noticed that the unknown gambler had picked the winner, number five, El Gitanillo.

I mentioned this to my son. "Do you think we ought to play his pick in the third race? Number three, Yves?"

My son studied the *Paris-Turf* and said, "The hell with him, and the hell with his pick, too. Yves hasn't got a chance. I'm betting La Belle Rive."

Well, it was only a five-horse race, and it seemed to me that this might be my chance to win back a lot of my lost money, because Yves was five to one, and La Belle Rive was seven to five. I went to the window expecting to bet Yves one hundred thousand francs to win, but I decided at the last minute to make it ten thousand win, ten thousand place. My son's horse took it in a photo finish from Zara II, Ruthenie, Delidy, and last came Yves. I was glad my son had picked a winner, and of course so was he. I was also glad I hadn't bet more on Yves. The man who had lost the program, or had thrown it away in disgust after the first race, had had the winner in the second, and I hadn't bet it, and he'd had the slowest horse of five in the third race, and I *had* bet it. So the hell with him, from now on I'd do my own picking.

In the fourth both my son and I agreed to play Mr. Sandman, and the horses finished Sky Top, *Mr. Sandman,* Ma Princesse, Takba, Tinca, Kakia, Tavino, Pipard, Haysti, and Merry Worden. Having bet Mr. Sandman to win and place, we broke even, but that's all. (You like horses, I hope. You like horse *races*, I hope. You like to read about bets made on them, I hope. Perhaps you have read *The Rocking Horse Winner*, and perhaps you have seen the movie they made of it. D. H. Lawrence. And of course this is *also* a letter. That is, to you. Therefore relax in your cell in the penitentiary and read the letter. It's from a friend.)

The fifth race was the big race of the day, the Prix Maurice de Nieuil, and you know who *he* is, six million francs to the winner, at a distance of twenty-five hundred meters, twelve entries, and my son said, "The winner is China Rock."

I believed him. The owner of the horse was H. G. Blagrave, the jockey was J. Doyasbere, the horse was out of Rockefella et May Wong, and I used to know Anna May Wong, years after she had reached the height of her career and fame. She was born in Fresno, or she lived there as a child, and Fresno was proud of her. And I have also always liked the name Rock. And last year I reached China for the first time, or at any rate Hong Kong. And all things considered it seemed to me China Rock was worth twenty thousand to win and ten thousand to place, but they came down to the wire Wildfire, Capitaine Corcoran, Silence, Bel Baraka, Argel, Exlio, Etwild, Tapioca, Blue Net, *China Rock,* Cassini, Jockero. The only other horse in the race I had liked for its name was Tapioca, but even if I had bet Tapioca instead of

China Rock, it would have come to the same thing, another loser.

"Now, look here," I said to my son. "Let's just lay off this anger and anxiety. We're here to have fun. If you can't lose without getting all worked up, you shouldn't bet. I want you to go to Harvard, but Harvard isn't going to do you very much good if a few losing horses can make you miserable."

"Baloney," my son said. "You don't like to lose, either. I'll go to Harvard if they'll have me, and I'll find out what I want to do, too—something in the arts, I suppose—but I'll pick the winner in the next race, too." And then, after consulting the *Paris-Turf* for two or three minutes, he said, "Jackson II."

I had reasons of my own for liking that name, so we both bet it, but the race finished Finaroc, Siky, Primeros Pinitos, *Jackson II,* Perseverant, Vatelador, and Cafougnette. Fourth, out of the money, *both* of us burned up about it this time. We decided to go up to the restaurant for the last race.

We sat down up there and ordered Cokes and ice cream, and my son said, "Well, it's King Cole and please bet *all* of this to win, nothing to place."

He handed me all of his money. I liked the way he was gambling, all or nothing, but I wasn't sure I didn't like Prince Aly Khan's horse Tantiery better than I liked King Cole, and so I urged him to reconsider, to handicap them again, to wait a moment, plenty of time. We ate the ice cream and drank the Cokes, and then he said, "No, sir, King Cole is the winner, that's all." That's when I noticed that the number-one horse had won the first race, and that this race was the seventh and last race, and King Cole's number was seven. I decided to go along with my son, and the hell with the Prince's horse. My son's money turned out to be eight thousand francs, which surprised him, since he had believed a five-thousand bill was a one-thousand bill. He accepted eight one-thousand-franc tickets on King Cole gratefully, and I said, "Well, you were almost even before you bet it all, you know." And he said, "The hell with even, I want to win, and this time I'm *going* to. King Cole is going to run them into the ground, that's all."

I liked this talk, it was the usual desperate wishful talk of the horse-player, but I liked it just the same. I had bet all of my own money on the same horse, too: twenty thousand to win, and ten to place. King Cole *was* in fact the favorite, the best bet of the day, too, as it is called, and it certainly appeared to be the logical horse to play, as the saying is. All the same it has been my experience that a long shot almost always wins the last race of the day, at least in America, and so I had certain doubts and reservations. At the break Vandris took the lead, with King Cole second by a little less than a length, and the rest of the field in a cluster about four lengths back. And that's the way it remained until they reached the stretch, when King Cole began to bear down on Vandris, and Mimmo and Mardochee left the rest of the field and came into contention. But you could see the power of King Cole.

61

You can tell which horse has got the real power when they are fighting it out in the stretch. King Cole drew up alongside of Vandris and they ran neck and neck for about forty yards, and my son asked himself in a loud clear voice, "Is he going to win?" And then King Cole moved a neck ahead of Vandris, then half a length, and then drew away by five lengths with only twenty or thirty yards to go. At this point my son shouted, "Go, boy, go." I laughed and said, "He's *gone.*" And then the race was over, and I reached out and put my hand on his head and gave his hair a little rub; he's going to go to Harvard, he picked the winner of the last race, and I had sense enough to go along with him. He was overjoyed. He better than doubled his money, and I almost doubled mine, because the place money was very little. We took a taxi home, bathed, dressed, and went to dinner at Maxim's, a big event for my daughter, a new event to write to her friends about. She kept the bill as a souvenir: twenty-one thousand francs, or forty-two dollars, but then, I drank a full bottle of champagne and they had three Cokes each, plus all kinds of good food, including crepes suzette.

CHAPTER EIGHT

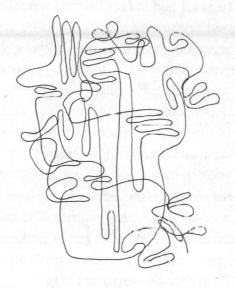

The Interviewer from Dublin said, "At fifty do you believe in your writing as you did when you were, say,
fifteen, twenty-five, thirty?"

"No, I don't."

"Do you believe in it at all?"

"Yes, I do, but differently. For instance, at fifteen
I believed that if I actually became a published writer,
an accepted writer, a writer with readers, my writing
would be a good thing for people. I didn't know how my
writing was going to be a good thing, I simply believed
that it was going to be a good thing."

"And then, at twenty-five?"

"When I knew I had in fact become a published writer, I still believed my writing was going to be a good thing, but I was beginning to wonder *how* it was going to make a real difference. There was already so much writing, first by writers who had finished their work and had died, and then by writers who had come through, as I had, who had become published, who had written for ten, twenty, thirty, or forty years, and were still writing. That is to say, I began to wonder about *all* writing, good and bad, by good and bad writers. Now, here was my own writing, my first book, a collection of short stories. Did this one book make a difference? Might it begin to make a difference later on, in ten years, for instance, or twenty? And if so, would the difference be worth noticing?"

"Well, since that time, twenty-five years have gone by. *Has* your first book made a difference?"

"A very small difference, but then the war itself has made only a very small difference. Everything always makes only a small difference. In short, we are who we are while we live, and after we are dead we are who we were, the dead are those who were not so long ago the living, and this in turn makes a small difference, but nothing much—to those who have survived, that is. There is no telling about any difference a living man may make on anybody, or on anything at all, by not dying, and then by not being able not to die any longer. Everything probably makes a small difference to and on everything, but it is probably never more than a very small difference. I suppose every man does his chosen work, or the work he is forced by something or other to do, for himself, for now, and not for others, excepting the few who are very near, members of his family, for instance, and not for later, although a writer, perhaps more than most others, is likely to be able to believe that what he writes this morning is for somebody tomorrow night, not excluding himself, or for a morning ten or twenty or thirty years from this morning. Yes, my first book has made a difference. No, it has not made the kind of difference that is worth noticing."

"Does this affect the writing you are doing now, or the writing you may begin to do tomorrow?"

"A little, I suppose, but not especially. It's my work. I believe I believe in work. A time always comes when it seems to be in order to work."

"I read your second book last week, and, as you know, it is a very long collection of short stories. I expected it to be out of date. I expected only to read around in it, but I found the stuff hardly ever out of date, and I read it from cover to cover. I understand the book was not especially successful when it came out, and it hasn't become successful in the meantime. I found my copy by accident in an old bookstore for a hundred francs, a great big book like that, but the man said that if the copy had been a good one, not a damaged one, covers gone, many pages coffee-stained, many torn and patched, the book would have been worth more than the original price. What I'm trying to say is that while I was reading the book, turning the worn, torn, stained, patched pages, I kept thinking, 'Hell, this is good stuff, some of this is great stuff. Is this what happens to writing?' And here you are, hungover and looking older than I ever expected you to look at fifty, and now I keep thinking, 'Hell, is this what happens to a writer?' Do you want to say something about this?"

"What can I say? Isn't it only a small part of a lot of other things? As far as I myself am concerned, the important thing is that *you* have survived, because if you hadn't, I wouldn't be talking to you now, I'd be talking to somebody else, and there would be *that* difference."

There were other newspapermen from other cities, and there were others who had come to Paris for a few days, and these others had also sat and talked. They had sooner or later asked questions, and he had answered them, because that's what we do. The best talk was late at night or early in the morning, sometimes at daybreak, when we were going good, after we had had a lot to drink, after we had gotten drunk, and then drunker, and then, still drinking steadily, had reached the sobriety that is deep in the heart of drunkenness, the sobriety of knowing, caring, loving, but somehow at last not regretting, or at any rate not especially regretting: the sobriety that impels the smile and transforms wisdom into love.

Now, therefore, let me tell about the book, my whale, so to say, or tiger, rock, tree, river, or sea, whatever you prefer. Not my own book, not the book I have written, am writing, will soon enough have written, but the book, the whole book of writing, of all writing, by all of us, and about all of us, for all of us, assuming we shall want to read, to go on reading for some time to come: assuming we shall go on wanting to know who we were at the time, what we did, why we did it, and how it made us feel and be. The book is *The Human Book,* or *The Book of Man,* which is another and perhaps a more accurate way of saying it is the Bible.

I began to believe we ought to have a new Bible when I was no more than eleven or twelve, but I didn't speak about it to anybody, certainly not to anybody in particular. I mentioned it now and then to pals who were sprawled out on the lawn of the Court House Park in Fresno, under a great tree, in the shade of it, on a hot afternoon in the month of August, but they didn't take to the idea, and I didn't try to make more of it than a little lazy talk added to the rest of the lazy talk of the day.

"What we ought to get ourselves is our own Bible, all about *us,* instead of about all those people long ago."

And one of the pals said, "Yes, and a little money, too."

The idea of the book wasn't pushed. I didn't feel like being pushy about it. I believed it was a good idea, but I kept noticing that everybody I knew, everybody I mentioned it to, was interested in other things. It didn't matter. It could keep.

The years went by, and at least two or three times a year I worked at the idea, jotting down a way of getting it to come to pass, and I spoke about it to somebody or other I happened to be speaking to about other things.

"The book we need is the book about us, now, not yesterday, and not tomorrow, either. We have got to have a new Bible, a new book for every home, every family in the world. We have got to get it written, to begin with, and that means we have got to choose our writers carefully and sensibly. We have got to begin by identifying God all over again, but that doesn't mean we have got to agree about the one God, or about any God at all. We have got to take all that we know, or think we know, which we know is very little, and we have got to begin with that."

Years went by some more, and then I began to write to publishers about the book. I had other work to do, too, other letters to write, but I found the time to write to publishers about the book, too. It was not my book, it was everybody's, and I pointed out that it ought to be written by everybody, it ought to be written by a great variety of men and women and children. A big part of the work of getting the book together would be to find the writers, and after they had written to choose from among the stuff that which was most right for the book. It would be a big book, but it would be one book, not two, or ten, or a hundred, or twenty-two thousand a year. The publishers replied and said the book didn't seem to be a possibility at that time, on account of the high cost of book production, or on account of labor conditions, or on account of other things.

The Gospel According to—you name him—the book had him, he was in the book, he had written his piece. Did you want to know the gospel according to an old man, perhaps the oldest man in the world? It would be in the book. He might say, "After being here a hundred and thirty-seven years this is what I know." And then he would tell you, and you could make of it anything you chose. You might want to know the gospel according to a great scientist, or a very rich man, or a criminal, or a madman, or a worker in a steel mill, or a wheat farmer, or a jockey—you would find it in the book, and the writing would be straight, it would be simple and direct. This would happen because out of all of the farmers in the world, for instance, a hundred or more would be invited to put their gospel into five hundred words or less, and then the gospel of only one of them would be chosen to appear in the book. If this seems a poor way to get such a book gathered together, just think of all the people who lived in the time of the Old Testament who *didn't* write or say or remember or live anything that appeared in that book.

Of course all of the books in the world *are* the one book, but you have got to have two or three square miles of library space to gather even a few of them together, and nobody in the world could ever read them all, even if he began at the age of seven and didn't stop until an hour before his death ninety years later. And what would he know? Surely nothing better than the fact that he had done a lot of reading.

From time to time the babel of the books makes me ill, and it happened again last night, my neck stiffening with the congestion of sorrow, meaninglessness, regret, anger, and love. Any time my neck stiffens I know the books have made me sick again. I know I'm being seized by uselessness, and it just isn't going to be easy to write, to add a little something to all the rest of the writing.

And it doesn't matter that I have no neck: my head seems to have taken a seat directly upon my shoulders about twenty-five years ago. My neck seems to have disappeared at that time, for I remember having had a neck in my youth. Sitting at a table and writing seems to have done it.

Whenever I'm writing, my kids want to know *what* I am writing, and I have got to say, "I don't know, but I know it's no good." This makes them laugh, but after a moment they seem worried, not so much about me, not so much about my writing, as about things in general, experience in general, art and truth in general, so then I say, "But don't worry about it, it's all right; every writer who *is* a writer believes his writing, while he's writing it, isn't good enough. But he goes on, because this is nothing new, and after he has done his work, after he has fought his fight, a fight *he* has provoked, a fight *he* has started, and after he has come near being knocked cold two or three times in every round, and has finished the fight all the same, and left the ring, half-dead and yet somehow happy, and he has forgotten the fight, or the writing, and then gone back to it, the stuff has not ceased

70

to be less than it ought to have been, but all the same there *is* something there, after all, there is a little something or other there."

Yesterday evening my son said, "I'd certainly like to read this book after you've finished it, if it's all right."

And I said, "Well, of course it *is* all right, but I think I had better read it first, after I have put it aside for a month or two, or a year or two, because not until a writer has read what he has written, and not until he has revised it, cut it, kicked out a lot and put in a little, is the book really written. The first writing is nothing more than the gathering together of stuff to work with, to shape and balance. There is a lot of stuff for you to read, and I don't mean stuff by me, although there is enough of that in print, too. This new thing isn't even a novel, you know. It's something else."

"Well, what is it, what would you call it?"

"It's writing. It's an essay, an attempt to find out if a work of writing can be achieved out of a special program that will somehow have both freedom and form, for as you may know I have for a long time been concerned about these opposites, I have wanted to find out if it is possible, for me at any rate, to balance them in a new work. Now, into this particular work, which had, and still has, an unknown identity, I have put as much freedom as I have had in me, but at the same time I have tried to put in form as well. I am failing, and before I decide how much I have failed, or before I decide it doesn't matter that I have failed, I must put the stuff aside, forget it, recuperate

71

from the fight, and then one day when I am restored go back to it, examine it, work at it, and then know for sure what I have, first, for myself, and then, for you, by which I mean for anybody, anybody *else,* who may be interested. By the time I am ready to go back to the thing, I shall no longer be only the writer of it, as I am while I *am* writing it; I shall also be the reader, I shall be you as well as me, I shall be the other reader, or anybody, and I may be situated by then in another city, not Paris, and in another country, not France, and in another time, not now. When you were very little I had to think twice about what I was writing, because I was a father, and I didn't know you very well, and I didn't want to write anything that might embarrass you—about yourself, or about me—but now that you are older, now that I know you better than I used to, and now that I know you cannot be embarrassed by any effort any man may make to achieve meaning, I feel free and I am able to believe you won't hold against me anything I may write. For instance, in this work there is some stuff that we might think of as being in bad taste, although it probably really isn't at all. It is easy for those who experience little to have contempt for those who experience much, and I don't mean to imply that I have experienced much, although I probably have, of a certain simple order, at any rate. In other words, the man who keeps his soul in a safe place all his life is likely to find fault with the man who has been unable or unwilling to keep his soul safe in the same sort of small place. You will get the hang of all this in another two or three years, most likely. In the meantime, I am simply doing my work, I am writing, and if the stuff is unlike anything else I have ever written, or a little unlike it, it is my opinion that that is in order. There are theories of wholeness, and I am not opposed to any order or theory of it, but I think that if a man has the ability or even only the compulsion to broaden the area of himself which he hopes eventually to make whole, he had better broaden it. The best writers stayed close to home, but I wish they hadn't. Let's take a couple of writers you know a little. Charles Dickens, for instance. Well, you know he wrote some of the most wonderful fables about the human experience any man has ever written, writing with a great and delightful style, full of a mixture of profound and almost inconsolable sorrow on the one hand and hilarious if sometimes hysterical joy and laughter on the other. Now, what I miss in his writing is some of the stuff that was in his life after he reached the age of twenty-one, for instance, some of the stuff that was his actual experience: his marriage, for instance, which soon became a mess, his affairs with other women, and his relations with his own kids, as against his relations with the kids in his stories, such as Pip in *Great Expectations*. Let's take also Anton Chekhov, another writer who mixed elegance of style with profound sorrow and magnificent humor—well, the poor fellow was sick his whole life, and although he was a doctor, he just wasn't able to fight off his own sickness. I'm not saying he hated the human experience. Most likely he did, as we all do, but at the same time he cherished it, too, but perhaps less, or at any rate differently, than most of us cherish it. My guess is that he decided before he was eighteen that he was dying, which is true, every man knows he is dying long before he dies, long before he is eighteen, too, and then Chekhov didn't do anything about it, he didn't do anything to postpone dying, to postpone the inevitable, he just wrote his wonderful stories and plays, he took a trip to Sakhalin to see how the people there were making out, and he went a couple of times to the south of France, to Nice, I guess, and Cannes, where I did so much gambling not long ago, and I believe he died there. Well, what I'm saying is, I wish Chekhov had found it possible or desirable to tell us a little more about himself, about his own fight, because he was a very rare fellow, a very special fellow, and it would do us good to know a little more about how he really was, how he really met the unattractive reality of each of his days and years, and all the rest of it."

A writer talks to his son, he talks to his daughter, he begins to write for them long before he has even met their mother, let alone married her, long before he has seen them for the first time and then seen them again and again from earliest infancy, through childhood, and on to full, or at any rate fuller, if not the fullest, identity. I talk to mine, at any rate, and after I have talked for five or six minutes, I stop for a moment, wondering about what the hell I have said, and giving them a chance to say something, too. Last night, for instance, after I had talked to both of them at the same time, my daughter hugged me and said, "Oh, Papa, you stink. Oh, what a smell you have."

Well, I do stink, so I don't mind having my daughter tell me so. She stinks, too, and she is as pretty as any little girl ever is, or ever has been. Our bodies make smells, depending on how we live, and don't we live the way that makes our bodies make *bad* smells? After she has had three Coca-Colas instead of a glass or two of milk, and two hot dogs instead of a couple of broiled lamb chops with a baked potato, her breath smells bad, but so what? Who cares about that? Kids are not flowers, they are early human beings.

"And then," I said to my son, "there are all the other writers, and I am thinking only of the best of them, the ones who really wrote, who knew how, and wanted to, and did. Well, they just didn't leave the several forms of writing in which every writer finds great safety, great security, great strength and balance, and they didn't move out into free language, out where the forms don't count, where the forms are a nuisance. They didn't tell us the things about the human experience we know they knew, and this makes me feel cheated. I don't want to continue this cheating. That's why I'm writing what I'm writing, a thing without form. I want to see if I can say how I live and work, have lived and worked and how I go on not dying, that's all."

CHAPTER NINE

The way it was yesterday is always what we want to know.

There was quite a lot of talk about Picasso between my son and myself as we rode to Fontainebleau. Also about George Jean Nathan and six or seven others, or was it sixteen or seventeen? It is sixty kilometers to Fontainebleau, and so there was a lot of time to use up on a nice afternoon, as the driver himself said.

The way it was, was that early in the morning I went straight to work, forgetting time, so that in an instant two hours had gone by and I had written eight pages. I was glad to have done that, glad to have gotten another day's work out of the way, and glad to be free again for the rest of the day. A touch of sweat broke out all over the place where I keep myself while I was at work on the last page, which might not have been the last page had the sweat not broken out, for the breaking out reminded me of the time and of myself, and I felt that I was tired, I wanted no more of work, no more of me, yesterday or thirty years ago, or a hundred, or now, or ever, all I wanted was to get up and forget, get out into the sun, walk away from where I keep myself, away from my body itself, walking in it and away from it at the same time, a free man, with his son beside him, both of them talking.

"Let's get out to a race track," he said, "and win ourselves a lot of money, because I know we can do it."

"Well, if there's a nearby track running, we'll take a ride out there and loaf around in the sun, because I'm trying to fight off this sickness, and the loafing in the sun will help, most likely."

But the only track running was Fontainebleau, and the taxi-driver told us it was about sixty kilometers out, a drive of at least an hour, he thought, and the round-trip fare, including his waiting time, was six thousand francs, or twelve dollars, so I put it this way to my son: "It's too far, it takes too long to get out there, Paris taxi-drivers don't know how to drive, the cost of the round-trip is fourteen dollars with the tip, it ain't worth the time and trouble."

My son put his reply this way: "Sure it is, Pop. Let's go."

I wasn't feeling too good in any case, I had other and better things to do, but I didn't feel like doing them, so we went.

It's a little track, something like a county-fair track in the United States, but the track isn't the important thing; the important thing is what we said about Picasso and the others.

"He charges too much for every little scribble and daub he makes," my son said. "He must be a millionaire."

"I certainly hope so, although I doubt it. He certainly doesn't force anybody to buy any of his scribbles or daubs. They've *got* money, and they want to buy, and the *agent* who sells the stuff sees these people, the buyers, Picasso doesn't, and the agent keeps a pretty good chunk of the money and hands over the rest to Picasso. Art is never a commodity on the market except to the buyers, and the buyers are always people with money who are out to get more money by hook or by crook, including a scribble or a daub by Picasso. He probably isn't poor, certainly not as poor as a lot of other painters who are in the last years of their lives, too, but he isn't rich, either."

"Oh, he's rich all right. At Maguy's I asked the man the price of a little poster with a few daubs added by

Picasso and a fresh signature and the price was seven hundred dollars."

"He doesn't sell many."

"They tell me his signature alone is worth more than a hundred dollars."

"You have this preoccupation with money, do you? Winning at the race track and how much Picasso gets for his signature?"

"Sure I have a preoccupation with money. Who doesn't? I don't want to be a bum, and if an artist hasn't got any money, he *is* a bum. UNESCO wouldn't have invited Picasso to decorate that whole big wall in the new building in Paris if Picasso hadn't been rich."

"Famous may be the more accurate term."

"Sure, but it means the same thing. Get famous and you get rich."

"Well, at any rate you didn't get the order garbled. A lot of people get rich but don't get famous."

"Willie Sutton did. He got rich first, and then famous."

"Willie Sutton *tried* to get rich by robbing banks, but it was his failure to do so that made him famous, not being rich, for he never was rich, he never made it, they always caught him, put him behind locked doors, and he escaped, until this last time, and now he's too old, he'll die there, reading the books he loves."

"What books are they?"

"Good books, for the most part. I wouldn't be surprised if he discovers Tolstoi in the penitentiary."

"Do you think he reads your stuff?"

"No telling, although he isn't likely to have been able not to stumble across something or other of mine in the course of thirty years of reading."

"I always liked Willie."

"I know. I wrote about it years ago, two or three days after I moved into the house on the beach at Malibu. The editors of a magazine called *Irish Writing* wrote to me from Dublin and asked me to write something, so the morning the letter reached me I sat down and wrote something, writing for four hours straight, which was what I called the piece, I think: *Four Hours for Irish Writing*. Well, in that piece, written in March of 1952, I mentioned our talks about Willie Sutton, but especially how much we both liked his reply to the police when he was asked why he robs banks."

" 'That's where the money is,' Willie told 'em."

"And the remark roared around the world, for it was one of the best ever made. Now that you're older, now that you've done a little time yourself, so to say, do you still like him?"

"Well, I do of course, but not the way I used to. I kind of feel sorry for him now, but in the old days I admired him, and I kept hoping he would escape again, but how can he, the poor guy, with everybody wise to all of his tricks, and everybody watching and waiting for him to try to make a little break? Poor old Willie's going to die in the pen."

"I wish he'd write the story of his life before he does."

"So do I, but does he know *how* to write? Just because

he can read doesn't mean he can write, too, does it?"

"Anybody who *wants* to can write. He can write one book, at any rate—the story of his life, as he knows it. Willie seems to be an honest man, and it would be interesting to know his life. He's not as famous as Picasso, and not famous in the same way, but Picasso never said anything more worth remembering than what Willie said. The artist and the bank robber *are* members of the same family. That is to say, they refuse to conform to the rules of the world. I call Willie a bank robber rather than a criminal because he doesn't seem to have gone about his business in the manner of a criminal, he seems to have gone about it in the manner of an artist whose art has taken the form of robbing banks. Now, when a painter tries to paint a picture and fails, he isn't captured, tried, and put in jail. He turns the painting over to an agent, who puts a price on it and tries to sell it, and sometimes does. Picasso wrote a play once, you know."

"Did you read it?"

"I read a translation of it, and I may say I enjoyed reading it, although it was very short, very affected, and very bad, but none of that mattered because it was this old man trying something new—for the fun of it, if for no other reason. The point is that anybody who wants to can write. Not a play necessarily, because that's a rather difficult form, especially for the amateur, but he can write *something,* he can put down a few words every day about himself. The important thing is wanting to. You've got to want to *enough,* or you won't, it will prove to be too much trouble. There won't be any other difficulty. Most people who think they want to be writers don't really want to at all; all they really want is to have something like that going for themselves, a nice big fat juicy excuse for not doing anything at all, much. How can anybody who wants to do *anything* not be able to do it? Such a thing is impossible. He does it, that's all. The reason I'd like to read Willie Sutton's life story, written by himself, is that I am sure it would amuse me."

"Is that *all* you want from a book?"

"Why? Is that too little?"

"I don't know, but I thought maybe you wanted to find out how he lived."

"Of course, and in finding out I have this feeling that I might be amused, and I need that, everybody does. Night before last, for instance, I began to read in the little paperback I picked up at the American Cathedral on Avenue George V six or seven weeks ago Paul's letter to the Romans, and this letter amused me. I had never had any idea what a lousy writer Paul was, I had heard that he had said some rather interesting things, but in the first six or seven pages of this letter to the Romans he was lousy, that's all. He didn't have a thing to say, really, he was just foaming at the mouth, blending equal parts of hysteria and fancy language, the same as Holy Roller preachers, only *they* really give you a good time, because they are so wonderfully stupid but at the same time so sure they have got the secret of everything by the balls, not to mention God himself. Now, I have made up my mind to pick up more and more of these paperbacks that churches are always leaving lying around on tables for people to pick up, and I am going to read every one of them straight through from beginning to end, because they are amusing. Paul says something obvious about human beings and how they live, and then he asks a question, and the question almost makes sense, almost implies that it's all right for people to be who they really are and to live the way they really do, and then he spoils everything by answering his question, and its implication, by saying, *God forbid*. His name was Saul until he left the religion of Moses for the religion of Jesus, but to this day you find plenty of proud Jews who go right on naming their boys Saul instead of Paul. He meant business, no doubt, he was on the level, no doubt, but he was a lousy writer. All people who believe something or other to the exclusion of doubt about all things have got to be lousy writers. What can you say if the answer is already in? For all we know, Willie Sutton might very well be one of our true saints, and if that's so, or even if it isn't, I believe it would be amusing to read his story."

My son said, "We ought to be in time for the second race, and the winner of that race is La Luge." I asked him to give me a rundown on the race, and after he had done so I said, "Well, his probable odds are only seven to four, but I'll go along with you, I'll bet La Luge if we get there in time."

"Should *every* bank robber write the story of his life?"

"*I'm* willing to believe that he should."

83

"What about those guys in their neat suits with their tight white collars who *work* in banks?"

"They should, too."

"What for?"

"Well, I might just come across one of their books and read around in it, and find it amusing, for one thing, and, for another, I have this idea that it would do every man in the world no harm at all to write his story."

"Well, would it do him any *good?*"

"It *might.* Something happens when a man writes no more than his own name, for instance. The fact that he writes it does something to him. Of course that's about all most people write, all their lives, excepting a few letters when somebody dies or is born. You can imagine what it might be like if a man thought about himself enough to try to put his life into words."

"Well, what *would* it be like?"

"Wouldn't it be like becoming somebody all over again, like being born again, almost, and like having everything happen again, only this time as part of a whole, like *wow,* as the jazzboys say?"

We bet La Luge. He got boxed in the stretch and drew up, getting up just in time to be last, but the races aren't what we are talking about. My son broke even, and I dropped a hundred thousand francs, but as I told him on our way back, "That doesn't mean a thing. You lose in one dimension, you win in another. God loves a loser, hates a winner, and doesn't bother at all about anybody who is never either."

"Why does he love a loser?"

"Because a loser knows."

"Knows what?"

"Knows he lost, at any rate, which makes him a little more real and true than he might otherwise be."

"Why does he hate a winner?"

"Because winning makes a fool of a man: it makes him think he's pretty good, that he can do no wrong, that he is one with God, which God doesn't like, and one with the universe, and a hell of a man with the girls, and all sorts of other things. It's happened to you, hasn't it?"

"How did you know?"

"It's been happening to me for forty years."

"Well, I can't be bothered about that, I like to win, that's all, and I hate to lose. But why doesn't God pay any attention at all to anybody who is never a winner *or* a loser?"

"It isn't *necessary* to pay any attention to him. He's just fine."

"Pop, you get these funny ideas about what God does and doesn't do, don't you?"

"Yes, I do."

"And yet you don't really believe in God."

"Not the way others do perhaps, but that doesn't mean I don't believe. Would I be a writer at all if I didn't? A lot of stuff we haven't identified we call God only because we have fallen into this habit of language symbols. It's a short cut, so that when we presume to speak about the enormous body of stuff we don't understand we won't need to talk forever before we are ready to say something simple about the whole thing. For instance, that we are open-minded about it."

"Are they going to give you the Nobel Prize for Literature next year?"

"What's that got to do with anything?"

"Nothing, but are they?"

"I don't want it."

"Not much, you don't."

"I don't."

"Well, suppose they give it to you anyway?"

"I won't accept it."

"Don't be crazy, Pop. You take that money and the honor that goes with it."

"No, I made up my mind last year. If they offer me the prize, I won't accept it. But don't worry, they won't."

"Why not? You deserve it. I ought to know. I've read just about every book you've ever had published."

"You haven't read every book all of the other writers in the world have had published, and there are a lot of them, writers and books both."

"So what? They can't write the way you do. Pop, you've got a way of writing that's different. Some of those stories of yours, I just can't understand how you ever wrote 'em. I can't understand how *anybody* could ever write 'em."

"Yes, you're quite right."

"And you always want to make fun of yourself, too."

"Who could possibly have a better right to do that? I know more about myself than anybody else does, and what I know just doesn't permit me not to make fun of myself—at least now and then. At the same time you know I am not disrespectful of myself. I read a story of mine the other night that came out in a new anthology, and I want you to know I was stunned by the indestructibility of the thing. I didn't really care *who* had written it. I was just glad somebody had."

He asked me to tell him the name of the story; I told him, and he said he would read it that night, but he didn't. I myself hadn't read it in more than ten years.

"Tell me about George Jean Nathan."

"He was the lordliest man I ever met, the only lordly American I ever met, and much lordlier than any authentic European lord I ever met."

"You saw him at the Royalton Hotel during the last months of his life, didn't you?"

"Yes, and it wasn't fun to see a lordly man like that brought down by disease. One afternoon he said, 'Not tonight, but next Monday, you come by and pick me up at seven and we'll go out on the town, like we used to.'"

"Did you?"

"Of course not. But of course I said I would. He was finished, and he didn't want to be. He'd had it, and it had been good, and this wasn't more of the same, this was something new. Everybody was astonished because he became a converted Catholic at the last minute, but why

87

shouldn't he do anything he felt like doing? He wasn't the same man, that's all. He gave the world the lord that he was, and he gave heaven the pitiful and helpless man he had become. The man who died wasn't Nathan at all."

"What do you mean, Pop?"

"You're always asking that question. You're fifteen years old now, not five or six or seven. I don't know what I mean, but I should imagine you might *guess*. Death takes a counterfeit every time, doesn't it? Especially when it takes a man who loves to bathe and put on fresh clothes and go out to the best places and dine and drink and have pretty girls at the table. Even when I was in the Army, he used to telephone and ask me to join him somewhere or other, and once he had two very pretty Chinese girls at the table, only they were passing, they were really Japanese, and we were supposed to have a couple of drinks and dinner and then go to the theater with the girls, but we forgot all about the theater, we just sat there and talked and laughed, and then we went to another place, and then to another, and pretty soon it was almost time for me to take a taxi to my outfit and stand formation at six in the morning. My brother-in-law's father was a barber in San Francisco during the Depression, and every now and then I would go to him for a haircut. I always had the money in my pocket, thirty-five cents, but he would never let me pay, and he always said it was a discourtesy to him whenever I got a haircut at another shop, so with money hard to come by in those days, I didn't mind paying him a visit now and then. I'll never forget the time I went in there and he nodded and began to give me a haircut, working hard and making it a good one. He was a heavy man who always seemed half-asleep and at the same time a little angry. During the haircut he didn't say anything, not because there was somebody else in the little shop or anything like that. He was working, and a lot of stuff had happened in his life, and he knew I was twenty-two years old and having a bad time, no money, no work, and no luck with my writing, but just before he let me out of the chair he said, 'Just remember one thing, please. You are going to be a great writer.' Four years later, when my first book came out, I inscribed a copy to him and took it to his new shop and handed it to him. He looked at the whole book, he read the inscription, he nodded, and he said, 'Thank you.' He said it very softly, and then he said it again, only softer. He nodded, I nodded, and I went out."

"Gad, Pop. How did he *know?*"

"Barbers *know*. Nish Papazian."

CHAPTER TEN

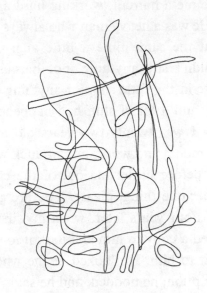

My daughter said, "Do you remember the donkey I thought I was going to have two years ago when we thought we were going to rent a house in the country near Barcelona for the summer? And long ago, do you remember the baby elephant I wanted? And the little ocelot I thought was a cat in the pet shop in Pacific Palisades, only the lady wanted seventy-five dollars for it? All my life I've wanted an animal, but now I guess it's too late."

I felt angry at myself for never having been able to give her an animal when she was little and wanted one: a pony, a horse, a baby elephant, a donkey, an ocelot, but that's how it goes, I guess. You just don't seem to be able to give a kid what the kid wants when the kid wants it, and after that it's too late. And then she remembered the eleven-year-old German shepherd, called Beau, given to her mother by an actor and his wife because they were going to Europe, and the dog would have to be put to sleep if somebody wasn't willing to put up with it. Beau lived in the same house with Lucy for a year, a noble animal with a touch of eccentricity. At last, it fell to me to take the animal to the place where old dogs are put to sleep.

"It broke my heart," I told her last night.

Now, as I shaved this morning, an hour and a half ago, I began to think about the time it takes for a writer to write a book. It doesn't come to a lot of time. For instance, if a writer writes for three hours every day for thirty-one days, and finishes his work on schedule, he will have worked ninety-three hours, which isn't very many hours. At ten dollars an hour, if he were working for wages, he would have earned nine hundred and thirty dollars, which isn't very much money, either. But this thinking didn't mean very much, it didn't mean anything in particular, it was only the thinking a man does while he's shaving, getting ready to go back to work, to put in another two or three hours at the typewriter. My son wants to learn to type. He thinks it was very sensible of me to learn to type when I was thirteen, because when he

91

sits down to type, it takes him two or three hours to get less than a full page written, and that's too slow.

"Can you type as swiftly as you want to? As swiftly as you *think*, I mean?"

"Yes, pretty much, although sometimes my thinking gets ahead of my ability to type. Still, I planned the whole business deliberately: to learn to type as quickly as possible, and after that to learn to write as quickly as possible. That is to say, to learn to write effectively; but only rarely has the writing been as effective as I have wanted it to be. You do your best at the time and under the circumstances, and you let it go at that, knowing you can have another chance any time you feel like it. My first writing was verse, you know. I won't call it poetry, because I have too much respect for poetry. Now, I expect to try verse again when I am old, I want the writing of verse, of poetry perhaps, to be the last work of my life, but there's no telling, I may find that I shall go along with the whole business pretty much as I always have, writing prose, as we call it, and now and then making another stab at the writing of poetry.

"Somebody writing a review of one of my books said that I was a poet *manqué,* so I tried to find out what *manqué* means, but for years I somehow just missed finding out. A few days ago, reading around in a French dictionary, I came upon the word, and it means *lack, want, shortage, deficiency,* and so on. Well, how am I to figure out what *that* means? What kind of a poet is a poet *manqué?* Especially if he writes prose?"

My son said, "Well, I liked the birthday poem you had in the *New Yorker* a long time ago, before I was born."

"Well, it's all right, most likely, but not really very much, a kind of kidding around, a kidding of the pompous human race, pompous history, and pompous poetry, too. The fact is that over the years I have published a dozen or more poems in a variety of magazines, including *Poetry* itself, which for many years was just about the only magazine that was earnestly concerned about poetry in the U.S. I got in long after the magazine had served its purpose and done its work, such as it was. There is a book called *Bartlett's Familiar Quotations*, and one of the last editions of this book was edited by the American writer Christopher Morley, a man who had liked my writing from the beginning. I was quite pleased when he included two or three quotations from my writing, but I was a little surprised that each of the quotations was from verse, of which I had published so little, and nothing at all from prose, of which I have published so much. But I guess it figures, at that, because the way you say stuff in verse lends itself to quotation."

And as I shaved, I thought about the title of this book, *Not Dying*. I wondered if it might not be something else instead. For instance, might it not be *All of the Days of July 1959* instead?

Every morning when I stop typing, when I get up from the table at which I work, one or another of these two, my kids, my son or my daughter, says, "Did you do your work? Did it go all right? How many pages did you write?"

And they are always pleased when I report that I did my work, that it went all right, and that I wrote six pages. They know I insist on not less than six pages every day, and so they are pleased when I make it. When I write seven or eight, they are especially pleased, although my son is a little unhappy about my theory that what I am writing is no good. So I have got to explain what I mean, which first of all is this: that the writing just naturally *is* very little, certainly not enough, a long way from what it might be, from what it ought to be, considering that I am now almost fifty-one years old, and have been a published writer for a quarter of a century, and an unpublished one for more than forty years. Then, I explain that any writer's writing has got to seem inadequate and useless *while* he is writing it, for the simple reason that he knows how much more it *could* be, if only it *would*. The important thing is for the writer not to quit—he has got to know and accept the truth about the stuff, but at the same time he has got to go on, he has got to finish what he has set out to do, he has got to keep trying, because if he doesn't, he won't have anything at all. If a man takes a wife, he has kids, even though he is not permitted to know what kind of kids they are going to turn out to be, he takes his chances, and it's the same with a writer. He writes, even though there is no telling how the writing is going to turn out. It certainly isn't going to be anybody else's writing, just as the kids he fathers aren't going to be anybody else's kids, they're going to be the kids of his wife and himself. A writer marries and he and his wife have kids, and at the same time he starts and finishes new works of writing. The kids grow, changing from year to year, but the works remain the same, but not entirely, for readers change and readers give a book its reality, even if the only reader of a book is the man who wrote it. There is no telling about either of them, kids or works of writing.

"All right," my daughter laughs, "disown me. I know you don't like me, so disown me. I don't care."

Your kids talk to you, they sass you, they have fun, and it's a great thing, but your books wait for you to change, to change a little more, never really changing very much, and they wait for you to read them again, to find out about them, and that is when you know for sure, or almost for sure, what they are, what you wrote long ago.

CHAPTER ELEVEN

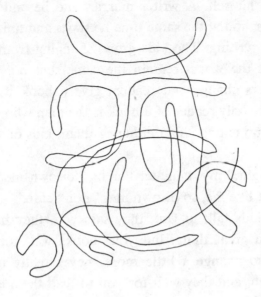

A writer gets letters from readers. Last week I got six.

This is from one of them: "Once upon a time, when I was in my teens, I gobbled up everything of yours I could find in the Public Library. Then came the period of critical awareness, and you descended to the bottom of the pile, where you stayed for a long time. On a second reading, though, book by book and story by story, you are moving back to the top. Now, I want to tell you a couple of things: how could you write so much good stuff and still write so much bad stuff? And why the hell hasn't your writing improved with age? So you owe the lousy Government millions, and you need more and more money, and the critics are eating your liver. So what? The Government will remain relatively solvent whether you pay up or not, and after you're gone nobody is going to collect anyway. And critics are habitual liver-eaters. But there are some people to whom you mean a hell of a lot, although you've never met them and probably never will. All the same, they believe in you. Like me, for instance. I think you're one of the best things that has happened to our writing since Mark Twain, and I think some day somebody's going to find this out and convince everybody else, too, but even if that doesn't happen, your good stuff will always be right there where anybody who wants to will be able to find it, and have it, and know it's great, that's all. But what a bum you are, to write so much lousy stuff, too. Why do you do it, for God's sake? Write something good again, will you? We don't want to believe a writer has got to go to pieces after he's thirty or thirty-five, forty or forty-five. Or kick the bucket, or go mad, or run off and hide somewhere. Don't write the way you wrote when you were a kid, but write something good again, that's all. There is still plenty of time. That little novel of yours about the guy with the tiger, for instance, that's one of the greatest."

Well, I wrote that little novel in 1950, in San Francisco, and I wasn't a kid at the time, either. I was over forty, and flat broke. And I didn't want to write at all. And yet, by way of reply to the writer of the letter, it is in order to make known that I decided to go to work, and to write, not one book, but three books at the same time.

I wrote all three in one month, in thirty-one days, and one of them was the short book about the guy with the tiger. In addition to the two longer books, there were to have been three short books, each to be written in ten or eleven days, but only the first one, the tiger story, was finished. The second one was abandoned midway, but I got around to it a year or two later and finished it, and the third one was abandoned after only three or four days. But the two longer works were finished.

I decided to write because my wish was not to write, and I wanted to fight off that wish, I wanted to find out if a writer can write even when he is shot, even when his spirit is a shambles, when his whole being is in ruins. I also wanted to find out if I might be able to earn the money I needed, and I needed a lot.

The books were published, but they were pretty much ignored by the critics, and that's all right, that doesn't mean anything in particular, although it did mean that the books didn't earn very much money, certainly not enough. They were flops, although each of them is gaining strength as the years go by, each is being published in different editions, and in a number of different languages, and each is finding new readers. These may be among the books the writer of the letter was thinking of when he spoke of bad writing, but the fact is that as far as I have been able to make out, the two books he didn't mention, the two that were written at the same time as the story of the boy with the tiger, *are* good books.

Now, on behalf of the writer of the letter, and perhaps on behalf of other young writers, it may be in order to make known how I worked at that time, how I got out the three books in only a month of time, in the year 1950.

First, the place where I worked. It was the study in my own apartment in the house I had built for my mother in 1939, an apartment meant to be a storage place for my manuscripts, books, correspondence, and other junk. A good big study with floor-to-ceiling shelves full of books, a first-class pianola, a radio-phonograph, and a fireplace. The worktable was solid oak, and quite old. I had had it from the time I had first moved into the apartment, at which time I had scraped off five or six layers of paint, and made it into a good-looking and very clean table, with a very smooth top on which to set the typewriter. I cleaned the typewriter and put on a new ribbon. I bought two bundles of typing paper.

A writer has got to have a good table, a good machine, and all the paper he is likely to need.

As I have said, I didn't want to write, but I knew I was going to have to, and so I got set. Getting set didn't take very long, either. It took one day, as a matter of fact.

I not only didn't want to write, I hadn't a thing to say: but *this* didn't bother me, either, because once a writer has got set to work, it has got to follow that something to say will present itself, for there is really only one general order of thing for any writer to say: us. This is who we are, like it or not, take it or leave it. This is how we live.

After everything was in order I put a fire into the fire-place and I sat and watched the fire. I get a lot out of fire. I burned stuff I found on the hillsides across from that house: branches fallen from eucalyptus trees, stumps, twigs, leaves, and other stuff of that kind. I smoked cigarettes incessantly, day and night. I was not about to go berserk, I had already gone, I had been there, I was there, I *was* berserk, but I was also intact, I was in my own study, and I had my own fire. I kept the thing roar-ing for five or six hours, and then at one or two in the morning I got up and stretched and shook my head every which way and held out my hands and shook them steadily for five or ten minutes, to get the blood racing back and forth, and I kicked my legs, and I got into the shower and washed away some of the poisons of my life, in my blood, in the sweat of my hide, and I said a prayer, the way fighters do just before the bell for the first round of a fight, only I didn't cross myself, I simply said, "Be with me, but if you can't be with me, if you can't help, then just don't hinder, either, and I'll be thankful." I got into the ice-cold bed and picked up a book lying on the top of the bed-table and I read for half an hour or more, and then I went to sleep. I slept four hours, got up, showered again, and then I did a lot of calisthenics, along the same lines as the calisthenics I did before I went to bed.

I went upstairs and drank three cups of black coffee without sugar, and then it was time to start. I went downstairs, sat at the table, put paper into the typewriter and began to write the first novel, beginning anywhere, and allowing myself not more than two hours in which to finish the first chapter. After that work had been done, I brushed my teeth to get the bad taste of too many cigarettes out of my mouth, and then I walked down the hill, walking slowly, to the Public Library in that neighborhood of San Francisco, called the Sunset, and there I looked at six or seven magazines, which I like to do when I am writing, when I am preoccupied with the unknown, with what is likely soon to *become* the known. Then, I left that place and walked in the streets there, through the village, as I called it, and I bought a loaf of fresh bread at a baker's, unsliced, and a paper sack of apples, and I walked back up to my house, where I had two more cups of black coffee, and then I went downstairs, sat at the table, put paper into the typewriter again, and began to write the second novel, giving myself two hours again in which to start and finish the first chapter.

After this work I brushed the teeth again, and went upstairs and ate a steak, and then an apple, and then I climbed to the top of the highest hill in that small group of hills, and from up there I looked down at part of San Francisco, at the houses all in a row, at the sea far away, at the Golden Gate, at the fine bridge there, and at the buildings of the city itself. I also looked at the different grasses and wildflowers and weeds and fallen leaves up there, and I listened to the faint sound of the wind moving among the leaves of the trees up there, and watched it play among the grasses, bending them, and I knew the arrogant loneliness of the writer at work, the old writer in the old fight, the lone man in the great contest with time and mystery. If I was mad, I was also free to heal the madness. The madness was private, my own, not public, and I was free to find out how best to banish it, and to become restored. At the same time, high up and alone with the grasses and the wind, I went over what I had started in each of the new works. I tried to guess where each was likely to go, and at the same time to wonder about the third work, which I had decided would be a short work, because that would make for variety, and at the same time perhaps I would be able to sell it to a magazine. As it happens, I wasn't able to sell it. Magazine editors are a pretty thickheaded lot, mainly, but that's all right: I offered it to only one of them, and then decided the hell with it. Now, when I had taken the first break, when I had gone to the Public Library, I had been away from my study less than two hours, and I wanted to get the amount of time for each break established; I decided an hour and a half would be long enough, but I was only an hour away from my work during the second break because I wanted to get back to work, to get the first day off to a good start.

Again, without thinking very much—you do your thinking long before you sit down to write, don't you?—and without making a false start, I began to write the story of the boy with the tiger. I began to write it? Is that accurate? Didn't the thing begin to write itself?

I was dying, that's all. I was sick, I was shot, I didn't know what I was doing, I only knew how to get my work-place in order, to get the tools of my trade in order, to get ready to get to work. I knew nothing at all about the work itself, the writing itself, except that I believed I would get it done, I would start it, keep it going, and finish it. In less than an hour the first chapter of the tiger story was finished, and I was free for the rest of the day and night, but I decided to just keep working, to take a recess, and then go back to work again. I was training, I was in training, for something or other, perhaps to become equal to anything still ahead in my life, anything more or anything worse, and to learn how to take failure, or even to transform it into something else, something possibly useful, even.

I began, therefore, a further work: a journal about the progress of the writing of these three works, and it was called (*More Later*), after the phrase at the end of incomplete news dispatches.

As soon as it was night I put a fire into the fireplace again, and I sat and watched the fire, the electric light of the room shut off so that I might see the fire from darkness. I watched the fire until I felt it was time for more calisthenics, and then I examined the mail that had accumulated, and I wrote replies to a couple of people. Then, I went upstairs and ate a bowl of yogurt with fresh bread, and that was the last of the eating for that day, the first day.

I wanted to eat as little as possible, because I was

loaded with fat, my weight was around a hundred and eighty-five pounds, and that's too much, that's all. I went downstairs to the worktable again, and a few minutes before midnight I began a new work for the months ahead: I began to write what I shall permit myself to call a poem. Precisely at midnight the poem was finished, and the first day of work was over.

I felt great and sick as a dog.

The pattern of work had been established. After that I got through every day in much the same manner.

When all of the work was finished, my weight had fallen to a hundred and fifty-five, my gut had shrunk to almost nothing, and I had ulcers. I didn't know it at the time, I only imagined that the burning there was from the cigarettes I was smoking, as of course in a sense it was. I found out years later that there were a lot of old ulcer scars there.

That's pretty much how it went, how I worked, how I wrote the stuff the letter-writer may have been thinking of when he wanted to know how I could put so much lousy writing with so much good writing. Well, you do it precisely the way you put the good stuff with the lousy stuff: it is the same thing, you do your best, and that's all you *can* do. It's better than not doing anything at all, isn't it?

Now, I'm in Paris, I'm not in San Francisco, I'm not writing three books at once, but I *am* writing this, working every morning, and after work loafing around with my kids, who are now well along into the lore of life and the world on their own.

CHAPTER TWELVE

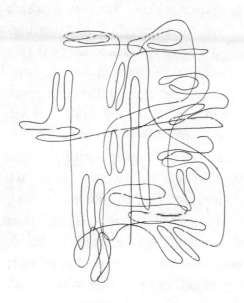

In sleep I saw a male lion seek out its mate in a valley far below where I stood on the porch of a house of some kind, a club perhaps, a public building perhaps, and just after the male reached the female, and they were beginning to consider one another, as all males and females do, across the valley a great elephant trumpeted rage and began to bound up the hillside on its way to gardeners working there, and on its way to the porch where I stood. The elephant was mad, and it meant to kill. It moved swiftly, trumpeting, and the gardeners dropped their spades and ran. When one of them fell, I said, "Now, where the hell are my kids? Are they in a safe place?"

I turned away from the fallen gardener and the charging elephant, not even waiting to know if he was able to get up and continue his flight in time to save his hide. I turned and saw my son aiming a shotgun, waiting for the arrival of the noble beast. My son's face was wet with tears, and he didn't mean to move until he had met the beast and tried to stop it—with fire that could do no more than irritate it. Before I could tell him this, he made his reply: "Well, maybe you don't care to try, but I do." He sobbed bitterly as he spoke, and the meaning of it was that he believed he was doomed, but he would be damned if he would budge from his place. And then, again before I was able to say anything, a man came running and said, "The elephant has been shot. It is dead." I went to the railing of the porch, and just down below, there was the elephant, lying on its side. A small man with a sharp knife had climbed upon it and was cutting through the tough hide and drawing it back, even while the elephant continued to shiver, moving one of its enormous legs swiftly, and then slowly.

And that was it, the sleep moved along, as it always does, to other stuff, which I don't remember, and don't need to. What does it mean? Who knows? It is a remembered dream, a small fragment of a man's early-morning sleep, and I put it here as simply as I know how because it was put in my sleep that way. Who put it there, and why, I don't know. I am asleep in a room in an apartment in Paris, and my son is asleep in his own room at the other end of the apartment. What have we got to do with elephants, with a mad elephant? Who knows, but who can pretend that he is not himself the elephant, which only now in sleep, ten million years later, is on the rampage, raging against a later form of itself? And who can pretend that he is also not the two lions, the one overtaking and the one overtaken, as they consider one another, on the verge of continuing the familiar procedure of using time together, emptying and filling at the same time, not knowing why, and then beholding new and smaller forms of themselves, out, true, and real—to appear again, much later, in anybody's sleep? Who can pretend to know for sure about any of it, any of us, all of us, which have eyes, blood, ways, and continuance? We don't know, we have never known, but now we understand the enormity of our ignorance enough to begin to feel obliged to reject all that we have so far agreed to accept, and to hang on, and to suspect, and to watch and wait.

I wanted to remember how this book had started, because it seemed to me early this morning that I owed it to myself to try for better form, better continuity, a fuller development of the several themes that were stated, or somewhat stated, at the beginning, but I just couldn't remember the themes, although I couldn't forget that one of them was the hunt—a man in the world hunting a woman. Well, that's what we do, isn't it? We overtake, as the lion does, and we do time together, that kind of time, that extraordinary kind of time, and out of this usage of time come more of us, who in turn shall use and be used by time and by the order and pattern which is there, and must continue. Women are a man's wives, all of them, or only one, it is all the same, and men are a woman's husbands, or her husband, the only one. All women are the mothers of the human race, and all men the fathers, and neither of them knew mothers and fathers who were mothers and fathers *alone,* or even at all, they knew who they knew, and it happened that out of all of the women in the world one of them was mother, and out of all of the men one was father, but both were also only a daughter and a son, and not especially effective at that, even—for it is not easy for any man or any woman to be *anything* especially effectively. It is not easy to be anybody's son or anybody's daughter, and it is even less easy to be anybody's father or anybody's mother, but everybody is one or another for a while. Lions beget lions, and they do it with a proper particularity, but in the end it is all lions, and so it is with humans: the male and the female of them beget the male and the female, and all men are sons and fathers, and all women daughters and mothers.

That's how I figure the dream.

Consider the whirling dervish, and do not scoff, for these orders of seeking to know deserve patience and respect. They do not come to pass for nothing, and it may only be an accident that the order of the whirler has had fewer disciples than the order of the crucified. The whirler reaches where he is to reach by whirling and by becoming less and less himself, less and less somebody lodged in his flesh, and it is the same in a sense with the crucified.

We are willing to settle for the little familiar details we know, which we have experienced again and again, and if we are willing to move these details around in new variations of the same book we have been writing since the discovery of writing, then of course we shall continue to have our books, and if the writer happens to be willing, and to have skill enough, these variations of the book must continue to comfort the reader. The book says this, the book says that. Now the name of the writer is Moses, now it's Mohammed. Now it's Plutarch, now it's Plato. Now it's Dostoevsky, now it's Dickens. Now Shakespeare, now Shaw. But the book remains the one book, the only book, and this is part of it, a chapter of it, a page of it, a word of it. And I do not mean to pretend that this part of the book is different, better, or something else special. How could I pretend any such preposterous thing? I am as captured as Moses was, as all the others were who lived, who spoke, who wrote. All I can say is you are you. And therefore you are all of it for as long as you stay, for as long as you are able to go on in the work of not dying, which is what this is about.

I was three hours yesterday doing my day's work. After which, unshaved, unbathed, I put on a shirt, a tie, and a jacket, and I walked a mile to buy a new typewriter ribbon. I took a taxi home and found them waiting for me. They had visited Art Street, as they call it, and my son had found a small pencil drawing by Picasso of a dove, with an olive branch in its beak, and the price was only seventy-five thousand francs, or a hundred and fifty dollars. Would I like to go and see it, because he wanted to buy it with part of his savings.

I said, "Well, I want to go and see it, of course, but if you want it, I want you to buy it, and not to have my approval first, because you no longer need my approval in anything you want to buy, or anything you want to do. All you need is your own approval, and that makes enough of a contest for any man."

"Well, I'd like you to see it," he said, "and if you can spare the money, lend me what I need until I cash a New York check."

We took a taxi to the little gallery, and I saw the picture and brought out seventy-five thousand francs and handed it to the woman there. I asked her to make out a bill of sale, please, mainly as a souvenir for my son, which she did, and then we left that gallery and began to visit all of them on that street.

In the street I said to my son, "I want to tell you how glad I am you found this Picasso drawing. It is one of his very best. It is absolutely priceless. You have a treasure now to take home to New York when you fly back early in September."

My daughter said, "Well, it *is* beautiful of course, but it isn't easy to *see*. The pencil lines are swift and very light, and you have to look hard to see what they are."

"All the better; it's a delicate thing, it's swift, it's like flight itself, you've got to look carefully if you want to see it at all."

My son listened to each of us, respectful of each of us, and then he said, "Do you really like it?"

It was almost as if *he* had drawn it, as in fact in a sense he had. And of course he has drawings of his own which are quite good, as good as the one he had bought, but he isn't Picasso, that's all. He held the framed drawing in the paper bag very firmly, and then he brought it out very carefully and stood in the street looking at it again, thinking hard, and then smiling with admiration and wonder. Where do you get as much for a hundred and fifty lousy dollars?

Now, the next day, he's back on Art Street looking at more drawings, looking for something by Matisse, and here is my daughter back from shopping, and she says, "Are you still working, Papa? Don't write any more. You've got six pages, haven't you? Don't write another word. I bought four boxes of raspberries and six peaches and I've washed the berries and cut up the peaches and mixed them together in a great big bowl with a little water and a lot of sugar, and it's all in the refrigerator. And I bought a pint of thick fresh cream, and pretty soon, when Aram comes back from Art Street, we'll eat some of it, the way we did last night."

Well, the way it had been last night was this: on Art Street I bought three big peaches, and the idea was that each of us was to eat one of them, but after I had eaten one, and had had quite a time of it, standing at the curb, the juices squirting all over, they had refused to eat one each, so I had brought two peaches home. Next door I had picked up two boxes of raspberries and I had made the same mixture my daughter has just made, because after supper, after the hamburgers we had made for supper, taking over the kitchen for a moment and driving the cook a little mad, because the kitchen, one of the biggest and best rooms in the apartment, is hers, we put thick cream over the mixture and ate it, talking about Picasso, and it was great.

For a while we encouraged the lady to cook and serve dinner, but she did everything wrong, and scowled all the time, and we ate the stuff anyhow, and after we had done so she always asked in French if it was good, and anybody should have known it was the worst cooking in the world. We wanted to get our own supper last night, so we did. Three big whopping hamburgers, a big ice-cold salad of sliced tomatoes, cucumbers, bell peppers, dry onions, and fresh parsley, and finally the raspberries and peaches with thick cream.

My daughter, at the glass door, says, "Don't write another word," so I don't.

CHAPTER THIRTEEN

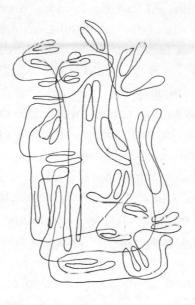

At Stanley Rose's bookstore in Hollywood about twenty-
five years ago there was a fellow who had worked in the
Pittsburgh steel mills and had written a number of short
stories about the Polacks and the Bohunks. He was a big,
hearty, loud-voiced, happy fellow by the name of Owen
Francis, called Hal by his friends. The stories he had
written had appeared in such magazines as the *Atlantic
Monthly,* and the *Saturday Evening Post.* But Hal hadn't
had a book published when he reached Hollywood
and began to look around for a movie producer who

113

might want to put him to work writing a movie about life in the steel mills. At last he found a producer, but he was asked to write about the intelligentsia of New York, which wasn't his territory, as he put it. All the same he worked for twelve weeks, and every week picked up a check for more money than he had ever before seen at one time in his life, a man in his middle twenties, eager for better food, better booze, better broads, and better fun, all of which were readily available if you had money, if you had a little importance, and if you were in the movie business. Like all of the writers who were going out to Hollywood from all over the country in those days, his declared purpose was to pick up some of the big money, hurry back to his proper place in the world, and write his first novel, which he expected to be something good. It is well known that few of the writers did what they said they were going to do, so it isn't necessary for me to dwell on that aspect of the matter. Very nearly all of the writers who went to Hollywood talked about the novels they were going to write as soon as they had saved up five thousand dollars, or ten, which soon became twenty, or even fifty. The more money you get, if you are a hungry writer, fresh from poverty, fresh from the cold of the grubby neighborhoods of the big cities of America, the more you believe you must have before you can write the great novel you believe you want to write. At first these writers talked about these unwritten novels, but after a year or two, after they had put away ten thousand, and then twenty, and a number of them fifty, and after they had run through half a dozen beautiful girls from all over the country with aspirations to be movie stars, and after they had bought homes with gardens, and after they had staffed their homes with Filipino or Chinese houseboys and cooks, and with gardeners, and chauffeurs, they not only talked about these unwritten first novels, they cried about them, and they blamed Capitalism for their failure to write these great books. It was a joy to visit the fine home of one of these writers, and to meet three or four of his friends, also writers, and to hear them all crying together about this outrageous situation into which they had been dragged against their wills. Stanley Rose himself was frequently on hand, and even while the writers wept he drank brandy and said, "They never had it so good, and they know it."

All it was was fun: the champion writers of the Hollywood studios, the writers of the screenplays of hundreds of the worst movies ever made, enjoyed gathering together and pretending they were martyrs.

But that wasn't how it was with this fellow from Pittsburgh. He was very happy to have the big money, to write the stuff the producers wanted, about intelligent people in New York, or about stupid people in Nebraska, it was all the same to him, and he was proud of the fact that he had gotten his first job on the strength of five short stories that his employer hadn't even read. Somewhere along the line, though, he had met Thomas Wolfe, and they had become friends. And all Owen Francis wanted to talk about was Thomas Wolfe and his writing, especially *Look Homeward, Angel.* Now, there *was* a writer —that Tom Wolfe, that giant of a man who sometimes wrote for three days and three nights steadily, in a kind of ferocious trance. There was a real writer, not a writer like these Hollywood cream puffs, not a phony, not a crybaby on his way to the bank with another week's paycheck for three thousand dollars, his gorgeous girl on his arm, keeping him from dying of loneliness.

"Hell," he used to say, "let's face it, I'm not a writer, and this easy work out here is just what the doctor ordered. I like to *read* good writing, but I know I can't write it, all I can write is a simple story about the poor slaves I worked with for so long, and the only reason the stuff I write is interesting is that I know it from the inside out. The background stuff is all true, and nobody else who knows that background can write at all, or wants to. My subject matter has a certain authenticity and appeal, but my writing itself is just plain routine and ordinary."

All the same, after about a year and a half of work in the movie studios, and a lot of fun, Hal found himself out of work, and his agent just couldn't find him a new job. And so Hal decided that, like it or not, he had better get the hell to work on his first novel. He had a little money stashed, but he knew it wasn't going to last very long at the rate he was going, so he put his typewriter on a table in his hotel room and he began to write the novel. The going was tough, first because writing had always been hard work for him, and second because he had gotten so

116

far away from where his life had been hard and real that he couldn't get the feel of it again. All of his Bohunks and Polacks had become members of the intelligentsia, or worse. They were all soft and glib instead of hard and inarticulate, as they had been when he had worked with them, as they still were, and as he himself no longer was. He kept after his work just the same, fighting a desperate fight, throwing away one false start after another, working from noon until dark, and then hurrying over to Stanley Rose's bookstore, and then going next door with Stanley and whoever else was around at the time, myself, for instance, to Musso & Frank's, first for three or four drinks at the bar, and then for a big supper, and all during the drinking and the eating, Hal would say, "Man, I'm trying, nobody can say I ain't trying, but I just ain't making it, that's all. And I've *got* to make it. It isn't that I have got to write a *good* first novel, it isn't that at all, I don't need to be a writer at all, but unless I write and publish a novel, I just won't be able to get another job in Hollywood, and I don't want to leave."

Every now and then he would say, "Well, it's going a little better at last. I got out three pages this afternoon that I think are the beginning of something halfway worth the bother. It's the first chapter, and I call it *Don't Laugh at Me, Mr. Boss*. You see, Bohunks and Polacks hate to be laughed at. Being laughed at, especially by the boss, is something like the supreme insult; it's like calling a man's father and his mother dirty names. And I never knew a Bohunk or a Polack who had been laughed at

117

who didn't go a little mad. Inside, at first. But from one day to another that dirty laughter grew in the poor man's heart and then you could *see* his madness, and you knew he might just kill somebody, but not necessarily the boss. It might be his wife instead—not the wife of the boss, his own wife, who had been taking a lot of beatings since the poor man had been laughed at, as if she were responsible for the whole thing. And he would beat his oldest kid, too, and the kid would believe that this was the way it was, that's all. He wouldn't believe this was wrong or different. His father was beating him lately, that's all. Well, that's the stuff I have got in the first chapter, and now all I have got to do is keep this stuff going until I have got a book written. In the last chapter I am going to have to decide if the poor man kills somebody—his wife or his oldest boy—or gets over his madness. So far it looks as if he's going to kill somebody, but at the last minute I may have him get over it. I saw it happen half a dozen times, and it's the gospel truth, but I'm not sure it's right for a novel, that's all. Do you want to know how he gets over his madness? Well, the boss notices that the man has worked harder and better than ever since the boss laughed at him, but he also notices that the man is ready to go berserk, and so the boss goes to him while the man is busy with his work, and the boss says to him, 'Nick, you are the best God-damn worker I got in this whole God-damn mill.' That's all the boss has got to do. The man is healed. His madness is gone. He gets drunk after work, he goes home with a new dress for his wife, a new shirt for his son, and he puts his arms around his wife and his son and all the rest of his kids, and they just don't know what the hell's happened to him—but I know. I saw it happen. Have I got a good story here?"

Stanley would say, "Sure you have. I got a man coming out from Scribner's tomorrow and I'll tell him about it. You write it and Scribner's will publish it, and then you can go back to work at a studio for big money. The book will make you five hundred dollars, but it *will* be a book, and I'll take it around to every producer in town and show it to him, along with the other books I'll be showing at the same time, and you'll be in again."

Well, Hal Francis worked on, and the going never stopped being tough, but little by little he got about half of the book on paper. The man from Scribner's sat with Hal and Stanley and a few of the rest of us who were loafing around the bookstore in those days, and he said he liked the idea and would speak about the book to Mr. Scribner himself. The minute it was finished, he was sure Scribner's would publish it.

I went back to San Francisco for three months, and then I got a ride to Hollywood again, and I began to loaf around in the bookstore again.

One evening Hal Francis came in and I asked him about the novel.

"What novel?" he said. "I can't write. Tom Wolfe can write. He's the only writer in the whole country. When a guy like that is writing, all the rest of us can put away our typewriters. Just take a look at his new book.

119

It's right here on the table." And he picked up a book and handed it to me. "Stanley just ordered a hundred copies more of the book. He sold a hundred in three days, and it's not even a novel; it's a collection of short stories, and you know short stories don't sell at all. *From Death to Morning*—well, take it, read it. Tom Wolfe is saying everything worth saying, and nobody else is saying anything. What's more, Tom's saying it the only way it ought to be said. He's bawling it out, shouting it out, roaring it out. He's got one sentence that goes on for three pages because he's a writer and he's got something to say, and you don't even notice how long the sentence is. It's that simple and that right, and the more you read, the more you know he's the only writer in the country, and maybe in the whole world. The rest of us nibble at little edges of life, but Tom sits down and eats the whole human race in two big bites, that's all. Ever since I read this new book, I just haven't had the heart to sit at my typewriter and try to write my silly little story about a Bohunk who has been laughed at by an idiot boss. About the poor man's poor wife, and his poor son, and the rest of his poor kids, and his poor madness. But Tom writes about the whole dirty human race and he transforms the sons of bitches into angels, all of them, even his dirty villains are angels, even they are immortal in Tom's writing."

Stanley told Hal to forget Tom Wolfe and write his own novel. It wasn't necessary for one writer to write like another. There was no reason for a fair writer to quit because there happened to be a better writer writing at

120

the same time. What Stanley wanted was to have Hal Francis in town, a nightly visitor at his store, because when he wasn't knocking his own writing Hal was one of the best guys in town to have around. In the end, though, Hal never finished the novel. He got a job with a producer again, but his pay-check was very small, and the job lasted only six weeks, and that was the way matters stood for the next two or three years.

Hal Francis and Stanley Rose met and drank and ate good food every night, going next door to Musso & Frank's, where they could afford to eat and drink, and Stanley tried to get his friend to finish his novel. Years after Hal had put the thing aside, despising it, Stanley was still up late at night, both of them drunk, urging Hal to finish the thing—he only had three or four more chapters to do—finish it, and get back into the big money. But one night Hal didn't show up, and Stanley went out to his place and found him sick in bed, and the next night Hal died.

"He died in my arms," Stanley said. "I buried the kid."

Well, now, Owen Francis was only one of the writers out there in those days, and what happened to him didn't happen to the others, or at any rate not to many of them, and certainly not in the same way, but the thing that killed the man, or helped do it, apart from the weight he had put on, and apart from the drinking he had done for years, was the fact that he didn't believe in his writing, *couldn't* believe in it. He believed that as long as Thomas Wolfe was writing there was no reason in the world for him to write, too. Tom Wolfe was saying it all. He loved and admired Wolfe as a giant of a man, voracious and insatiable, a compulsive writer who was also inexhaustible, or very nearly so, and he loved and admired him as a writer, a working writer, a man who stayed in a dump of an apartment in Brooklyn, who worked with such intensity that he forgot time, forgot food and drink, and then after long hours of fierce and trance-like concentration and the swiftest writing in the world, and sometimes after a whole day and night of it, and sometimes even more, he staggered out of his hovel, his huge body purified by the fiery labor, his heavy body made light, almost weightless, by the passing of the hours, and he began to fly over the streets, crossing the bridge to Manhattan at three or four in the morning, finding men at work on the docks, joining them in their work for an hour or two, and then flying on. Tom Wolfe was a soul, he was a spirit, an angel in a huge human body, and his old friend Hal Francis believed that he himself, equally big and almost equally voracious, was nothing and nobody, and had nothing to say. Well, of course Hal was mistaken, at least a little, about Tom, and he was mistaken about himself, too. He *had* something to say, and he said it often enough, but not in writing. He said it at the bar, drinking. He needed somebody to listen to him *now,* and not later, and the best ear he had was the ear of Stanley Rose, a new friend in a new part of the world.

CHAPTER FOURTEEN

What *is* a writer to say that hasn't already been said?
Why, he is to say the little *he* has to say, and it doesn't
matter how little this little may be. *He* is to say it, and
say it again, the same as each of the writers have said
what they have had to say, little or great, saying it over
and over. And what *did* they say? Well, not really anything at all, actually: always more of the same, of course,
with the name of the male changed, and the name of the
female changed, but each of them the same as all of the
other males and females ever written about, each of them
alive for a time.

As a small boy I believed that the piano might be able to do something for everybody, but I just didn't know the language of music, and so I couldn't put it to work, and I couldn't learn to play the piano the way I believed I ought to learn: suddenly, swiftly, totally, with the fingers knowing their way to absolute truth, to every sound of truth that was in me. And so I left the piano to the piano players, although I myself preferred the player piano, the pianola, and the playing that came from the rolling roll, and from the electric motor. If words can't carry us to grace, can sounds, music, silence?

And so, once, after I had done a number of plays, after I had written them, after I had directed them, after I had seen them, I decided my next play would be one in which nobody would say one word, and yet it would not be a mime play, if that's the right word; it would not be an eccentric play, it would be perfectly natural, and its meaning would be clear and unmistakable, and greater than the meaning in any of the plays that were full of words, full of people working their lower jaws, their tongues and teeth, their vocal chords. I kept thinking about this play for weeks and months, and then, God help me, I forgot all about it.

But I think it was a good idea, and I pass it along to any playwright who may find out how to do it, for I am sure that it can be done, even though I am not in favor of starting a cult of silence, of nonspeech, in the human race. We had our chance in that dimension, and we lost it. The eye is enough if we happened to be willing to be simple, to permit ourselves to grow in simplicity, but that is impossible for us now. We want more and more, and this illusion of being able to have more and more, this unproved theory that there is more to be had, is able to persist on account of words, on account of language, and the expert or inspired use of it. But *is* there more to be had, and, if so, what is the nature of this more? Hadn't a number of the wisest men, all of them old by then, discarded one thing after another until all they had was themselves, or what was left of themselves, and a hard floor on which to lie down and sleep, a plain garment in which to be loosely clothed, or at any rate covered, a bowl out of which to eat the very simplest of food, a spoon, and nothing, or very little, else? Hadn't the wisest of us put aside the junk and trash of the world, rejecting the whole illusion and theory of more? But a new life wants more, a kid wants more, a young man wants more, and almost everybody wants more all his life, whether it's a short life or a long one. But what is the true form of this more that is so desirable, that every man never stops trying to have? Is it spirit? Well, too much spirit is very difficult to cope with. Is it matter? Well, too much matter makes for fat and sickness, and finally death. Is it death, then? Well, death is the final uselessness, the final order of it, and the final form of meaninglessness. So what is the true form of the more which man believes he must have? Is it peace? Well, peace is no more than a moment that follows turmoil, and without turmoil there can be no peace, and if there *is*, then the man is mad, his peace is madness, and what good is that? Is the desired more balance? Well, balance is at the heart of all things in any case, isn't it? There is nothing in the universe that is not delicately balanced, and not subject to sudden imbalance, and if the first is inevitable, so is the second, and one cannot be more desirable than the other. So what the hell is the order of the more that we believe we have got to have? Time? Well, there is no end to time in any case, and don't we know it? As far as we know, whatever time is, it has always been, and it will always be. Is it ourselves we must have more of? Well, we are forever discontented with ourselves, aren't we? So how could we want more of that which discontents us, which we really do not know, cannot really like, and would like to forsake in favor of something better, or at any rate a little less unattractive, foolish, troublesome, impure, improper, stupid, ridiculous, pompous, fearful, sickly, and so on and so forth? What is there for a writer to say? Man, I was there, wasn't I? Is that it? Man, you don't know me, and you never will, I've been dead only a minute now, a hundred years now, but I was there, wasn't I? I had that body and I lived in it in the place for a while, didn't I? And didn't I breathe in and breathe out for years, and didn't I eat and drink and talk and have fun and love and hate? Didn't I tie my shoelaces tight and go out and walk, and didn't I look and look? Wasn't I the one, though, even as you are the one now, reading this, and not yet gone, not yet out of it once and for all? Is that what a writer is to say?

Let me tell you this. Day before yesterday I went with my kids by taxi to a little street across town, on the Left Bank, and there we visited a little store in which for two hundred francs you can put a machine to work making an abstract work of art for you. The machine works for three minutes. A metal finger at the end of a metal arm clasps a piece of colored chalk: press a button and the arm moves up and down and from right to left, and makes marks on the white paper. Press another button and the machine stops. Remove the chalk and replace it with a piece of chalk of another color, and start the machine again. Stop it and put another color to work, and after three minutes you have got a work of art, all for yourself. My son discovered the place, and brought home two examples of what he had achieved, and he urged his sister and his father to go there with him, and give it a go, too, and so we did. We each made three machine abstractions, and the man there rolled them up and put a rubber band around the one big roll, and my daughter carried the roll, but when we got home we didn't have the roll. We had stopped to buy peaches from a pushcart peddler and we had put the roll on the ledge of a building and we had left the thing there. Well, we didn't like that, so the next day we went back there to see if the roll was still there, but it wasn't, it was gone, somebody had found our machine art and had gone off with it, and the stuff was priceless. The stuff was great. We lost it. We felt awfully angry at ourselves for losing what we ourselves had made, and we got into a little street argument about where to go next, but the argument ended when we found a marble game, and took turns running up a score. My daughter's score was the highest: two million, nine hundred thousand, plus three stars, all of which meant something, although we didn't know precisely what, and in any case the game cost only twenty francs a crack, and paid nothing, it was just for sport, but for an hour there, at the entrance to that saloon, we had ourselves a time, forgetting our loss. When I say we played the marble game, I mean my son and daughter played it, while I stood at the bar and drank a cup of very hot black coffee, on a very hot afternoon. Why not? Man, there we were, a hell of a family: my son with the famous scowl of his father's family, and the angry annoyance of a great man with all things, of a man who doesn't yet know by which means to reveal to all the world his greatness: writing, drawing, painting, composing, or what? And my daughter with her narrow face and her dark swift eyes, and her joy in all contests, including art: all she has got to do is see her brother making a watercolor, and she buys her own set and her own paper and she makes ten of them to his one.

And all she had to do was watch him run up a score of nine hundred thousand, and there she was running up a score of *two million* and nine hundred thousand, plus the three blinking stars. And didn't her father say to her, and to her brother, "Hell, this girl is a genius, that's all. She can do anything anybody can do, and she can do it swifter and better, and she isn't even interested in a career in art, or in beating the marble games; all she wants to do is marry a good boy. Baby, you are the greatest, you are the joy of my heart."

Let me tell you how it was, what we did, and let me let it go at that. We know there isn't anything to say, don't we? We know nothing we say or do is better than anything else we may say or do, don't we? So what do we care? We were there, weren't we, and wasn't it great? Hell, we came to a narrow street where the Arabs had opened shops and didn't we go into one of them and look at the junk in there? Wasn't that our immortality for a moment? We bought a bag of unshelled peanuts and shelled and ate them, didn't we, walking down narrow streets in Paris on a hot day of July in the year 1959? And don't ever forget, brother, that it all started away back in 1908—for me, that is. It started earlier for my father, and later for my son and daughter, but for me, starting in 1908, and still being abroad in 1959, in Paris at that—man, you know it means something: it means me, it means I was there, and if there is another meaning to anything, to any of it, anywhere, you write and tell me about it. I'll be waiting to hear from you. Or somebody else will be waiting. And even if he doesn't so much as suspect it, I will be more of him than he is, just as I am not able to suspect that Columbus (for instance) is more of me than I am, although it is the truth, and not the big fat lie it seems to be at first glance.

Man, you have got to keep looking. Not twice, not three times, but a billion and three times, and then again, one last look, because it is always that last look that gets it. I am here, I was there, man, where are my feet, where are my arms?

CHAPTER FIFTEEN

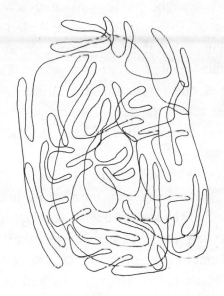

My kids were kidding me on a walk up Avenue Victor Hugo yesterday afternoon, and they said, "Do you know, Pop, you know everything."

I said, "Let me tell you this. I know when it rains, but I don't know why, although I would try to find out if I thought it would help."

Whenever my kids and I get our own supper, my two hands appear to become four, because I want to get to the food while it's still hot, and for other reasons I can't think of at the moment. My kids watch and laugh and say, "Hungry?"

There is a photograph of Matisse in a book in French that my son brought home yesterday afternoon, and in the picture Matisse is holding a cat with a serene face. He is an old man, and the cat is an old cat, and they have done a certain amount of time together. They are not strangers, and one suspects that Matisse loves the cat. A man takes after art, after drawing and painting, and fifty years later he finds that he loves the cat.

Who do we love?

We love our kids, or at any rate we love the idea of them, even before they are born, even before we see them for the first time, even before they are able to demonstrate who they are, or at any rate we love them some of the time, wonder about them some of it, and hate them some of it, because they are our own and no more than we are. We love them and notice that they hate us, perhaps more often than we hate them, and we wonder about that, too: we are who we are, and they are who they are.

The other day when I ate a peach standing at the curb my son was ashamed of me, and later he said, "Honest to God, Pop, when I see you acting like a pig, like when you were eating that peach, I wish you weren't my father."

I said to my son, "Well, now, I don't mind about that at all. You *ought* to wish you had a better father, but this is the father you have. Be your own father if you want a perfect one. A peach isn't an easy thing to eat, and I happen to enjoy eating a peach in the street. You've got

132

to work swiftly or you'll lose more of the juice than you ought to lose. Working swiftly, you have got to be nothing more than a pig for a moment, but how long does it take to eat a peach? You read D. H. Lawrence's little poem about the proper way to eat a fig. You read it the other day in the bookshop where we stopped a moment to look at the books in English. Well, it wasn't a bad little poem, but the fact is there is only one way to eat a fig, and that's with your mouth. If the mouth belittles us, that's too bad, but whether we eat daintily or not daintily, we eat with our mouths, and it comes to the same thing. You can repudiate me as your father any time you like, and perhaps you should, but don't forget that it works both ways, and I can repudiate you as my son, too, thus repudiating my own father, a man I never knew. And what's the good of that? We are all of us stuck with one another. We are all we have. Trade places with me, be my father, and the situation is still the same. It has got to happen sooner or later, in any case."

My son said, "You don't have to take every little thing I say seriously, do you?"

"Who *says* I don't? Do you expect me to suddenly stop being interested, just because I am being provoked by my own son instead of by the children of others? That would be a pity, wouldn't it?"

Summer's almost gone, winter's coming on, and the next time I clear my throat and hawk into the street, making a noise that shocks my kids, it will be another time and another world, and I will have failed.

133

And my daughter's astonished that I stink. I tell her I work and sweat, and in the summer sweat stinks.

"Well," she says, "what's the matter with using a deodorant?"

And I say, "Ah, no, not that, the very word stinks worse than my sweat. I have never used a deodorant in my life, only soap and water, and I'll be damned if I'm going to start now. I don't take pills to stop a pain because I want to know *when* I have a pain, and the nature and duration of it. And I don't try to hide my smell, because I want to *know* when I stink." Who do you love? Yourself? Your children? Your father and your mother? The whole human race? That savage and corrupt family?

In the window of a small bookstore near where I had eaten the peach I saw a copy of a book called *The Theatre of Bertolt Brecht,* so I went in and bought it for three thousand francs, or six dollars. At the top of a stack of old books on the floor I saw a copy of one of my books, so I bought this book, too, for one hundred francs, or twenty cents. The Albatross Press: Leipzig, Paris, Bologna, 1938, twenty-one years ago. I had first seen the book in the month of July 1939 in Paris, and I had examined it carefully, although I didn't read any of the sixteen stories in it. And there I was, looking at the book again, my two kids beside me.

Jim Tully told me the joy of his life as a young writer was to arrive in a new city and go to the Public Library and find his books on the shelves, but where can you find them now?

And John Fante, in the secondhand bookshop on Sutter Street in San Francisco, standing among the great stacks of old dusty books, turned suddenly and said, "For God's sake, let's get out of here. This place makes books seem like so much dirt."

My daughter whispered, "Tell her you wrote the book, Papa."

But I couldn't do that. I had done it long ago.

When my first book came out I took it around one whole afternoon and showed it to people and told them it was my book, I had written it myself.

"Tell her," my daughter whispered.

My son whispered, "Ah, shut up. She *knows*."

Going out, I saw a copy of my first book, in a new paperback edition, in a wire rack, and I asked the woman how much it was, and she said six hundred francs, and I said, "That's a dollar and twenty cents." But I didn't buy it, I only examined it, and it looked just fine, all new and bright, and then I put it back in the wire rack, and we left the shop, and my daughter said, "Why didn't you tell her? If I were famous, I'd tell everybody."

"Ah, shut up," my son said, and they gave each other the dirty looks they have been giving each other ever since they began to talk.

"It isn't necessary to tell her, it isn't necessary to tell anybody, and I am not famous."

"Well, then, who is?"

"Nobody, of course."

The name of the first story in the *Albatross* book was

135

The Sunday Zeppelin, but I couldn't remember when I had written it, and the name of the last one was *Where I Come From People Are Polite,* and I *could* remember. I wrote it in the little front room of the family flat at 348 Carl Street in San Francisco away back in 1936 or 1937. I enjoyed writing that one. The surprises that came in the writing pleased me and I broke into laughter two or three times before the story was finished. But I haven't laughed once in the writing of this book. And it isn't that there isn't anything to laugh about any more. There is more than ever, as a matter of fact. And there is more simple gladness in every day I reach than ever before in my life, too.

I tell my kids suddenly in the evening after supper, "Are we lucky? We've got good health, our digestions are good, we enjoy eating, and we've got this cool apartment, and a big bedroom for each of us."

My daughter says, "Let's go to a movie, then. Let's go see *Viva Zapata.*"

So we go out into the cool of the evening and we begin to walk up Avenue Victor Hugo, toward the Arc de Triomphe, and it's great to be out there, walking and talking and laughing, remembering people and how they spoke to us earlier in the day.

We go to the movie; all of the seats are the same price, but the lady with the flashlight at the top of the center aisle starts flashing it on and off, blocking our way.

"What the devil does she want?"

"The ticket stubs, the ticket stubs," my daughter says.

"What for? The seats are all the same price."

My son says, "Pop, will you please give her the ticket stubs, and stop disturbing the whole theater."

I go through my pockets looking for the ticket stubs, I find them at last, I show them, and the woman leads the way.

When the movie ended and the intermission started, another woman selling ice cream came down the aisle and I said I wanted three. Vanilla.

"Noisette? Chocolat? Pistache?"

"No, Madam, vanilla."

Again she ran through her list, and again I said, "No, Madam, vanilla."

My kids began to be annoyed because people around us were listening and watching, and my daughter said, "Take chocolate, Papa." But I wanted vanilla, my daughter wanted vanilla, she had said so when I had asked if she would like some ice cream, and my son wanted vanilla, so again I said, "No, Madam, vanilla."

And then the woman said, "Vanilla! *Oui.*"

And she handed me three of them, and all I wanted to know was why she hadn't done so in the first place. Vanilla is vanilla in French as well as in English, and I kept saying the word in the French way every time, so why didn't she choose to understand in the first place? Did she want to find out if I could really speak French? Well, how much French do you need to chat with an ice-cream peddler in a movie?

My kids accepted the ice cream with annoyance, and

137

I said, "What are you sore at me for? What did I do?"

And my daughter said, "Papa, you are impossible. You get so angry at everybody. You speak so loudly. Everybody listened and watched."

"Well, that's too bad, isn't it? From now on go to the movies alone. I saw the picture when it first came out. I only came because I don't like you to be in a place like this if I'm not around. This place is full of creeps."

"O.K.," my son said. "We're old enough to go to the movies alone. You don't like movies anyway, and this one you hate. What's the matter with it, anyway?"

So we argued a little about the movie. I like to encourage them to argue, I like to notice their earnestness, and their annoyance with me, the everlasting fault-finder, the loud-mouth. Did anybody in the world ever have a more impossible father, did anybody ever have a father so fatheaded, arrogant, stupid, and just plain nuts? But pretty soon, in the midst of the argument, they find something to what I'm saying, and they decide to look into that a moment, they ask questions about that, and so little by little we become friends again.

After the movie we walk up the Champs-Elysées to the American Drugstore where we have chocolate sodas, and then we walk home, taking our time, and talking and laughing all the way, knowing how lucky we are. Every hundred yards or so we see a streetwalker, and now and then we see a man stop to chat with her, and my son says, "The other night one of them smiled at *me,* for God's sake. For a minute I thought I'd stop and speak to her."

And my daughter said, "You wouldn't dare."

And my son said, "Oh no? That's what you think."

And even this pleases me, even this is us out there in the streets.

But the days grow short, summer is almost gone, this book is almost done, it's almost written now, and I don't like it, it isn't the kind of book I believed it was going to be.

When all was quiet in the house, I picked up the book about Brecht, because I had heard so much about him, and I wanted to see if I could find out what it was that he had, and I read around in the book, and looked at the photographs in it, but all I could gather was that he had been born in 1898, and he had died after about sixty years. He seemed to like to write about the United States, even before he had ever visited the country. He seemed to be all out for change, and of course that is always a good thing, but he seemed to believe the proper or only way to achieve change is by means of violence, and maybe it is, at that, although the change you get from violence doesn't ever seem to turn out to have been change at all; it always seems to settle back and become more of the same, and how did it happen that he never noticed that, or, if he had noticed it, how did it happen that he never made anything of it? Was it too tough to make something of it? Did it make the achieving of exciting drama more difficult?

What change?

When I reached Russia in 1935 I expected to see a new human race, because everything there was now *for* the people, *all* of the people, but it wasn't so at all; everything was exactly the same as ever, and that was when I began to be bothered about the theory of change. Who changes, and how? The clever are always the clever, the others are always the others. I have had arguments with my son about a number of rich Americans we both know and he admires and I despise. He doesn't like my contempt for rich men who get richer when there is a war, for instance: men who don't get drafted into an army, and don't get pushed around like so much cattle. He believes the war isn't their fault, why shouldn't they go right on being money-making businessmen during a war? I explain that by going right on they become killers, that's all, and I cannot respect men who are unwilling or unable to understand what their useless money-making means, and what it is doing. He studied civics and history with an idiot teacher at an idiotic private school last year, and he remembers some of the things he was told, and he uses these things in his arguments, but it is no use: I despise any man who makes money out of human disaster. Well, did Brecht achieve his fame because he wrote down to the multitudes, all the while knowing better, disbelieving the theory of change he pretended to cherish, writing up a little to the few half-baked and articulate people a playwright needs in order to appear to be great?

CHAPTER SIXTEEN

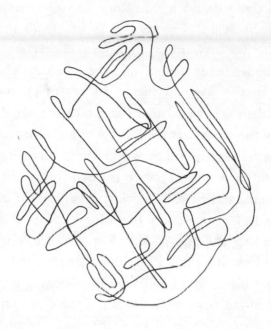

When I began to write this book my theme was the end, the unwilling coming to the end, or not dying. Very soon the book began to move this way and the other, and I began trying to keep it to a straight line. Now, while I cannot say that all is lost, I have *got* to say that all is entangled, *again* entangled. I was bursting with health, or (if you prefer) with ill-health. I was alive with much the same intensity I had known when I was fourteen or fifteen, restless and sleepless. There was nowhere to go that I could believe would make a difference, and so I stayed where I was and sought to make a difference on my own. Ivan Bunin in his story *The Gentleman from San Francisco* and Thomas Mann in *Death in Venice* put themselves forward as the central characters in these stories, under other names, and these central characters were men who were in the midst of travel, men who were on their way to another place on the map, although in reality the place was death. There are other stories of this sort, written by other writers who have lived long enough to know and to notice the two forms of travel in dying men: exterior and interior, geographical and spiritual. And of course every one of us notices this all the time, reading our newspapers. For instance, only a few days ago I sat at a sidewalk table at the corner *bistro* and sipped hot black coffee and read the morning paper, and came upon the news of the death of the German painter George Grosz only a few days after he had returned to Germany for the first time since 1939. Had he gone back to die? Had he known this, or had only the death in him known it, and kept it secret? He had done his best painting in Germany before the war, revealing man as a kind of pathetic monster. This fierce view of man was satisfying, not because his man, his human race, was German, but because his vision was true, and his skill great. In America, though, he began to paint differently, his vision changed, and his work lost its angry reality. His pictures became very nearly pretty, because he didn't want to be ferocious about the Americans, he wanted to be kind about them, and kindness just wasn't the way for him. He taught painting at a number of schools here and there, but one can imagine that his heart wasn't in it, as it wasn't in his new paintings, either. His place was Germany, but he had had to get out of Germany, and thus out of himself, too, which no man is likely to be able to do gladly, or effectively. At last he felt the time had come to go back to Germany, to himself, and he had done so, and he had died.

Ten years ago I sold a story to the editor of a big magazine, and he asked me to have lunch with him, so that we could discuss the story. I walked three or four blocks from my apartment on Fifty-eighth Street in New York to the building in which the editor had his offices, and we took an elevator to an upper floor of the building, where we sat in a private dining room and were served an excellent lunch. We discussed things in general for fifteen or twenty minutes, and then the editor said he would be happy to pay me thirty-seven fifty for my story. At first I didn't understand what thirty-seven fifty meant. I had been paid fifteen dollars for my first short story, but that had been fifteen years earlier, the magazine had never earned any money, and so I had been happy to accept the small payment, but surely this rich magazine, with a circulation in the millions, was not offering me thirty-seven dollars and fifty cents for a story. It took me about fifteen seconds to realize that he probably didn't mean thirty-seven dollars and fifty cents; he probably meant thirty-seven *hundred* and fifty dollars. Now, I had hoped to be offered at least a thousand dollars for the story, which at that time, when money was so scarce, meant a lot to me, and so I was tempted to accept the offer immediately, but I decided I had better wait a moment, and thereby perhaps avoid being unwittingly unfair to myself, and to the story. After all, it *was* at least twice the length of most short stories, and I was quite sure that he had frequently paid even more to other writers for a regular short story. Thus, it did not seem unreasonable of me to expect more for this one. I said I felt the story was worth five thousand, whereupon the editor remarked, "O.K., you've got it."

I was glad I had taken the time to think about the whole matter, and hadn't accepted his first offer, because with five thousand I could pay a lot of debts and forget money problems for a little while. The editor said he didn't mind that he wasn't paying other writers as much as he had agreed to pay me, because he felt my story was worth the money. He said the last time he had paid so much for a story, the writer of the story was one of the most famous in the United States, and in the world for that matter, and of course he mentioned the writer by name, which I have chosen not to do, for a reason that will be clear in a moment. The editor then began to discuss the latest novel by this writer, a novel he had bought for an enormous sum, and had run in three successive issues of the magazine. The novel had been bitterly attacked by the critics.

The editor said, "Well, he wrote the thing under the impression that it was his last book. He had been told by his doctors that he had a disease that was fatal—no need to mention the disease, although it was a clean one, if that matters—and that at most he could expect to live not more than a year. He used up what he believed to be the last of his time writing that book. It is full of death in a way that just isn't quite right. I happen to like it, but I know it isn't his best. And then, after he had finished the book, it was discovered that his illness was *not* fatal, was not in fact what his doctors had believed it had been, and he was as good as new again. But he *had* written it when he had believed he was as good as dead."

Around Christmas-time last year, 1958, I myself began to get messages in my sleep and even during wakefulness, messages *from* myself, or from whatever it is that we call ourselves, and these messages tried to tell me that my time was up. And I tried to accept the messages with grace. I didn't run to a doctor, because I have the peasant's mistrust of doctors, and because I believe death is something between All and the dying man, it is not something between doctors and the dying man. The messages did not stop, or the meaning of them change. My time was up, they said.

"O.K., so my time is up. What do you want from me?"

I longed desperately to see somebody I loved, but most of the ones I loved were dead, and the others were far away: that is, my kids. But I knew I couldn't expect very much from my kids, because kids belong to both sides of the human race, they belong to a mother, and they belong to a father, and when these two sides are separated, when a mother and a father are divorced, kids themselves are separated in themselves, and if they live with the mother, and if the father sees them only now and then, as I had done for ten years, they don't quite know him. And of course I didn't want to bother them about myself, although the intense loneliness made me feel I ought at least to see them, speak with them, take them to dinner, embrace them, and go about my business. I thought I had better wait and watch some more, though, first: another day, another week. Hadn't this sort of thing happened before? It hadn't.

And I wasn't sick, either. I was entirely sound, and not in despair, either, although little by little I began to notice that my spirit was hushed, and I didn't enjoy getting out among people. Consequently, I decided to force myself to do that, but every night the moment I turned away from the people, I was home again with this enormous and impersonal truth of death.

The year ended, and I decided to get out of there, and start waiting somewhere else, anywhere else, because if I was going, I might as well go, I might as well travel, too. I even remembered the stories by Ivan Bunin and Thomas Mann, and I even thought I might as well understand that this journeying was inevitable in one form or another for every one of us when it is time to go. I had a very bad time getting my junk packed and stored, for nothing is more pathetic than a man's accumulated rubbish, all kinds of bright things which have faded, which he cannot bear to discard once and for all but must put aside somewhere safely. I came upon papers I hadn't seen in thirty years or more, drawings, small paintings on typing paper, notes for stories and novels and plays, and all sorts of abandoned works, and I just *had* to glance at each of these items for the first and last time, it seemed to me, and this was painful and stupefying. At last I decided to just dump the stuff into the heavy cardboard cartons provided by the storage company: not to look at anything, let it go, forget it, and get out of there.

The secondhand Cadillac I had been driving for two years I gave to a friend, and I got on a train, because I wanted to have another look at the country from the window of a train, and I traveled from California to New York. I saw my kids, and as luck would have it my brother was in New York for a few days, so he went to dinner with us, too. During dinner he spoke of our meals at home, and my son's eyes sparkled, and my daughter smiled, and I thought, "Well, I guess this is what it comes to. This is my brother, and these are my kids, and we are together, years later, at a table, eating and drinking, and soon everything will be different again, a lot different."

I was back at the hotel where Nathan had died, and I was back in the city where my father had first set foot in America, in 1905, alone, my mother still in the old country with my two sisters and my brother, this man of fifty-three at the table with me and my kids. My father in 1905 was on his way to a new life for all of us in the new world, or so he believed, at any rate. And here I was just about finished with that new life in that new world, and on my way back to Europe, to the old world, to the old life.

I had at first believed I might linger in New York indefinitely, but soon I knew I couldn't do that, I had to keep going, and so I looked for money by means of which to keep going. I found it, and I went.

When I went aboard the ship, and when the ship began to move away from the dock, down the Hudson into the Harbor, past Ellis Island and the Statue of Liberty, I believed I was on my way to my death, that this was my last voyage. And that is the point.

All the same, I had plans, and I *believed* in the plans, too. I believed I would make a moving picture in Yugoslavia, and when I knew that this was not to be, I believed something else. I believed I would drive to Switzerland and find a house there and buy it, and bring my kids over and put them in good schools, but when I knew that that was not to be, either, I believed I would go to Spain, to Valencia, and live in the sun there, but I didn't go to Spain, I went to Aix-en-Provence, where I believed I would win at the casino, but I didn't win, I lost. And then I went to Nice, where I lost some more, and to all of the casinos on the Riviera, where I lost, and then I believed I would go to Paris, and write and earn some money, and I went to Paris, and I wrote, and I earned some money.

I got the money just in time to fetch my kids from

New York, and just in time to rent an apartment, and something did come of it: July.

And with the arrival of July came something more: the need to use up the time of July in the writing of a new book, this book, about not dying, for that is what I have been doing since around Christmas-time last year when the messages began to come to me. Not dying is not the same as living, it is only a little like living.

One day a friend of mine tracked me down all over town to the office of a lawyer I was consulting about my taxes, and he said, "Can you come up here right away. I think I'm dying." I took a taxi to his hotel and found him sitting with a girl of the streets, drinking whisky at four in the afternoon, both of them drunk, and he poured me one, and he said, "What am I going to do? I *know* I'm dying, and I'm scared witless." I sat and drank, and we talked for about an hour, and then I suggested that we meet again at nine and have dinner, and we'd talk some more. At dinner he said, "For three years now, ever since that dirty heart attack, I keep thinking I'm going to get another one, and it's going to kill me like a bullet in the head, and I don't know what to do. What shall I do?"

Well, what could I tell him? He was not even fifty, he was only forty-seven. I didn't know what to tell him, so I said, "How about gambling? Have you ever thought of that as something to do?"

He had, he said, but he had never gambled very much, although he'd like to try, so we went up to the Aviation, and he took a place at the *chemin de fer* table, as I did,

149

and soon the hours were going by unnoticed, and he was ahead almost two hundred thousand francs, or four hundred dollars. We got up and cashed in our plaques and put our money away, and we went to a little night club nearby where girls liked to loaf and drink, and two of them joined us, and the next day he was a little embarrassed about the telephone call he'd made, and he said, "Hell, if I'm dying, who isn't?"

CHAPTER SEVENTEEN

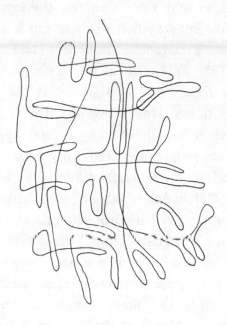

Heavenly Father, you may have noticed a series of articles in the *Saturday Evening Post* under the heading of *Adventures of the Mind,* of which there have been thirty-one so far, the thirty-first being by Bertrand Russell, which he calls *The Expanding Mental Universe*. And years ago you may have noticed a piece of sculpture by Noguchi called *Miss Universe Expanding*.

You may also have noticed year before last all of those thistles growing along the railroad track from Trieste to Zagreb, straight up to a height of about five feet, sometimes six, with as many as two dozen arms, each arm with two or three thistles at the top, each plant being a whole congregation of these noble and flawless thistles all along the railroad track from late afternoon to dark. Didn't the sight of them please you, make you feel glad, and a little lonely and scared at the same time, since these things are throwaway things, accidental things, which have happened again and again without any help from people, and frequently with considerable interference from them. And yet there they were, hushed at nightfall, mainly unnoticed, or only swiftly noticed by somebody on a train. I tried not to miss any of them on my side of the train, but I know I missed ten times more than I saw, for it isn't possible to see every one of them clearly when there are so many of them and the train is moving so swiftly. One time, though, the train stopped, and I had a good look at the nine of them that were there directly beneath my window. And didn't you, too? Weren't they something? Weren't they really more than anything else anywhere else, almost?

And wasn't it about twenty-five years ago that a horse named Miss Universe appeared in the turf world of America, and never won a race? Wasn't it at that time that a horse named Gift of Roses ran and won a number of cheap races, and another named Panther Rock, and another named Earl of Warwick? Well, what I mean is, you surely saw their names up on the entry list at the bookie's on Third Street, where Alabam and Fat Fagin used to work for the syndicate. You may even have seen

152

the whole big back room full of gamblers, making half-dollar bets, including the Norwegian house-painter who talked about Ibsen all the time. What happened to the Norwegian house painter? Did he die? Did you ever see a more earnest and sorrowful man? And what about the accent he spoke with? Did you ever know a more earnest, courteous, and decent man? Did you ever hear anybody say better or more important things, and say them more simply?

Now, there's that great big popular five-cent American magazine that for ten or fifteen years has been selling for fifteen cents, and here all of a sudden comes a thistle by a railroad truck. Made you feel good, didn't it? Made me. I read the first *Adventure* and rejoiced, because *there* was a thistle if I ever saw one, there was a talking thistle, a writing thistle, and not a flaw in it anywhere, not a speck of cheating in it, all straight, all designed for un-assuming glory. I rejoiced and said to myself, as you may have done, too, "Well, now, this *is* something. This is going to get it, maybe." This is what all of the thistles have been waiting beside all of the railroad tracks *for*, this is the moment of the thistle, and isn't it a far better one than the moment of the moon, the moment of the rose, the moment of the crucifix, even, begging your pardon. This is better than pie, this is better than peaches and cream, this is silence with its thoughtful voice, blind-ness with its gentle glance, truth without its arrogance, and didn't you think so, too? I did. And then I waited a couple of weeks, and there was the second *Adventure*, and this time I thought, "Oh, boy, the thistles are speaking at last."

I saw them from the train to Zagreb. I felt that I was looking at my own soul, and I hadn't ever before felt anything of the sort when I had looked at anything else. I wanted to read every *Adventure* in the series, and after that I wanted to write my own *Adventure,* and didn't you, too? One thistle wrote about religion, if you'll pardon the expression again, or about believing, and another wrote about meaning, and another about thinking, another about the animals, another about energy, another about time, another about this and that, and another about the other, and didn't I say to myself, "I've got to do one about everything, because I've got the ignorance for it."

That's exactly what I said, as you may remember. But I didn't sit right down and start to write my piece. I waited some more, and I continued being right where I was, where I had always been, by the railroad track, not on the line from Trieste to Zagreb alone, not on the Lackawanna line alone, not on the Rock Island line alone, but on all of the lines all over the world, and all of the lines out of the world, which you understand so well I feel almost ashamed to bring it up. I waited because I wanted All to be quite a bit. I guess I have got to want a thing like that when it comes to a thing like that. All. That's why I started with the horses, because you know they are a thunder, and a wonder. Where else except in a horse do you see so much thunder and wonder mixed together?

Now, the reason for this little prayer is that I want to tell you again that even though I have been writing for forty years, and even though everything I have ever written has been a prayer, and even though I ought to have learned something about writing after so many years of it, I don't know how to write. Now that I want to write about All for the series in the *Saturday Evening Post,* before the editors suspend it, I still don't know how, I don't know where to start, and you have surely looked at those very small white flowers that grow in lawns? Well, what about them? I can't leave them out, can I? But if I try to put them in, I don't know *where* to put them in, and I don't know what they are called, either. I'm not asking for help, I'm just letting you know what a difficult thing it is for a man to write about All. Try it sometime and you'll know what I mean. Or have you tried it? Rough, wasn't it? Now, I know you've been reading the series, and you must have learned a few useful things. I did. I learned to laugh, for one thing. I mean, differently, in a new way, didn't you? Sure you did. Not at anybody, and not with anybody, either: just laugh, like Army psychos with athlete's foot do all of a sudden in the middle of the night, and then call out your name and ask if you're awake, and if you are, tell you, "How about the wow, man? How about the great big everlasting wow? You remember the California wow, don't you, the same as I remember the New Mexico wow? Doesn't that old wow make you remember and laugh and remember some more and laugh some more until you can hardly stop?"

You remember him, don't you, old Laughing Boy from the Indian reservation in New Mexico, with his athlete's foot and peace whoops? He'd done his war whoops, and by then, if you remember, he was doing his peace ones. You heard him say, didn't you, "Man, I believe in wow with all my heart and soul, because I know if it wasn't for wow in the beginning and wow in the middle and wow all the time I would have been blown to pieces the same as a lot of other Indians I know. We're Christians, you know, some of us, but we're wow Christians, or we're dead Christians, and wow is better than dead any day." You heard him talking softly all night, didn't you? I did. Laughing and trying to keep it soft, and trying to stop, and talking softly, all about the wow religion. What happened to *him?* I can't even remember his name, but I'll never forget when he called out from the truck that was hauling him to the airport, and from there home, "So long, Frisco, see you in New Mexico." And waved and waved as long as he could see anybody standing there in the cold January wow of a bleak and dismal Army hospital road, not in a field somewhere, but in the great city of Paris itself. Where does a stupid writer start in a piece about All? What do you leave out? Whose death, even, can you leave out? Can you leave out the deaths of the Christian Indians who weren't wow Christians? Of course you can, and do, as you know. Nobody cares about the dead. They're *dead,* what can you do about them? You have got to stick with the champ, the living, no matter how they managed to make it, no mat-

156

ter who they fooled to keep the title. I want to write about All, the same as I wanted to in 1917 when I wrote an essay about money and its effect on people, the same as I did in 1918 when I began to write philosophy, the same as I did in 1919 when I wrote about murder, and the same as I did every year since then, but so far I haven't done it, I haven't known *how* to do it. Do you remember a story somebody published in a magazine away back in 1921 that began, "The sun shone brightly through the window onto Harold Watkins's face." Well, what about this fellow Harold Watkins? Did you ever know him? I never did. I never knew *anybody* on whom the sun shone through the window. My people were always in the shade when they were asleep, unless they happened to be living at the Garden of Allah in Hollywood, and even then, even there, by the time the sun was moving through the rosebushes they would be up to adjust the Venetian blinds and keep the sun out. Even so, any writer who wants to write about All can't leave out Harold Watkins, can he? We know Harold Watkins had a face because that's what the sun shone on. Who can write about All and leave out Harold Watkins? Or anybody else he remembers? Or anything else?

What I mean is my own memory goes back to the time when Gift of Roses was running in the sun; how much further back your memory must go, and what an enormous confusion of sunshining you know about that I don't. I'll bet you saw a lot of melons ripen on a lot of vines along about the time Watkins was waking up, and a lot of butterflies, too. Maybe you remember one little white butterfly with orange spots on its wings one morning in the month of July in Oakland, California, in the year 1911, moving among three or four dozen butterflies of the same kind. I do, and I kept my eye on that one butterfly until he got all mixed up with all of the others, and it damn near broke my heart. Did it yours, too? Because he was the one I was watching, the one who was mine, and then he got lost in the crowd. A kid doesn't like that, do you? A kid doesn't like anything he believes is his own to get lost in a crowd, and everybody is always getting lost in a crowd. You say so long to a pal and watch him disappear among people in the street and you feel he's disappearing forever, getting lost among the crowd of the dead, even though you know he's only on his way home to supper, and it hurts you, doesn't it? Does me. And then you come face to face with a girl you have never before seen, eleven years old to your twelve, and she's walking with her mother, holding her hand, and she disappears into a department store, and you know you'll never see her again, because she just died and was buried in the department store. Can you write about All for the *Saturday Evening Post* and leave that out? How do you pick and choose? All is all, isn't it? Are the bees watching us? We certainly have been watching them for a long time. And the horse races, and the thistles alongside the railroad tracks, and the newsreels, but what else are we supposed to be watching, but don't even *know* we're supposed to be? We've looked everywhere, haven't we?

We've followed all of the expanding, haven't we, as far as we *could* follow it, making the universe so enormous that this whole planet is no more than the equivalent of a grain of sand on a beach that moves a million miles in every direction, and what have we got for our trouble? What have you got for yours? Athlete's foot? Wow? Have you got wow, as we have? We haven't got justice or anything fantastic like that, but we have got wow, and while it isn't much, certainly not everything, it's a lot better than nothing, and it is inside of everything we know, everything everybody has written about in the series in the *Saturday Evening Post*. I want to put wow into everything, into All, but I know I never will, and you know why, too. You're stuck-up, that's why. You don't want anybody to have All, or to understand All, you just want everybody to have a good time for a little while, that's all.

CHAPTER EIGHTEEN

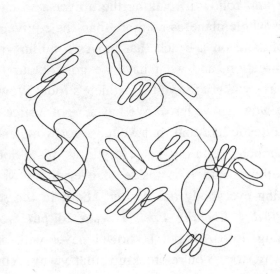

The *Paris Review* is published in Paris, but the magazine maintains editorial offices in New York. It is published in English, and comes out four times a year. In every issue there is an interview with a writer. The magazine also publishes drawings, generally by artists who are already famous or by artists who have a new style.

If you are around fifteen years of age, a magazine like the *Paris Review* can seem to be a much more important affair than a magazine like the *Atlantic Monthly,* for instance, because the magazine is new, it is young, and so are you. The magazine's most important feature is the interview, under the heading of *The Art of Fiction*. Everybody who reads the magazine believes there is an art of fiction, as of course there is, and the publisher, Sadruddin Aga Khan, and the editors, George A. Plimpton, Peter Matthiessen, Donald Hall, Robert B. Silvers, Blair Fuller, John Moseley, Eugene Walter, Elizabeth Faure, Louise Bruce, Louise Fox, Gillian Goldsmith, Ann Kadinsky-Cade, and Irene Urdang, not to mention the advisory editors, Thomas H. Guinzburg, Harold L. Humes, Ben Johnson, Archibald MacLeish, John Phillips, Pierre Schneider, Max Steele, William Styron, and Francis Wyndham—all of these are continuously on the lookout for a new writer to be interviewed. A tape-recorder is put to work, so that the interviews will be both conversational and accurate.

I was at the George V Hotel in Paris, about four blocks from the offices of the *Paris Review*, at 16 Rue Vernet, when a young American, born in Paris, and just lately back from six or seven years in California, suggested that he might borrow a tape-recorder and that I might find the time to answer his questions, on behalf of the magazine. I was writing a play at the time, and I didn't want to talk about writing, but I said we might do the interview later on, after I had finished the play. In the meantime, did he know my books, because if he didn't, that might make the interview more interesting. Unfortunately he knew two of them quite well, three or four others fairly well, and he was trying to catch up with all of them, so that he might better be able to hit upon a suitable scheme for his questions.

"For instance," he said, "I have an idea it might be a good idea for my questions to be about other things than writing itself."

Yes, I told him, that might be a very good way to go about it.

He said, "I would like to ask, for instance, how you see things, how you look at things. Do you give them only a glance because you have already seen them so many times, or do you look directly at them *again,* as if for the first time, and if you do, why?"

I told him to go right ahead in that direction. He went off after that first discussion in the lobby of the hotel, and he came back a week later for another talk, this time at a table in the patio, just off the lobby, where I urged him to order melon, but he preferred two or three cups of coffee, as I did.

This time, among other things, he said, "I have been wondering why anybody at all ever became a writer in the first place, and while this is a question that is very definitely about writing, it isn't exactly about the art of fiction, so perhaps you won't mind if I include it among my questions."

I agreed that this new question was a good one, but I urged him not to let his scheme keep him from asking a question about the art of fiction itself, if he felt like it. He said he had been up to the offices of the magazine and had spoken with somebody there about his idea for an

162

interview with me, and he had been encouraged to go ahead.

I said, "Well, I finished the play day before yesterday, and so from here on in whenever you're ready, I am."

He went off again, and a few days later he telephoned and said, "I am trying to borrow a tape-recorder. I will telephone again very soon."

He did, and then he came to the hotel, but there was still stuff to talk about, he said, so we talked. He wanted to know what I thought of the other interviews in the series, and I said I thought they were O.K., not because they revealed anything important about the art of fiction, but because it is always interesting to read a question, and then to read an answer to the question. Any question will do, any answer will do: it's the form that's appealing. Plays about people in the courts have always been popular on that account. A man who is about to be executed is always asked, "Have you anything to say?" Well, who *hasn't?* But in this case the question is rude, as there just isn't time for anything like an adequate answer. And yet the question is asked as if there were all the time in the world, as there is for all the rest of us, and especially for writers. The wonder of it is that anybody about to be executed has had the ability to say anything at all on the one hand, and on the other that nobody has taken the question literally and made an appropriate reply. Nobody, for instance, has talked for longer than a minute, and almost everybody has said all that he has had to say in three or four words. Many have replied in one word, No, and even more haven't replied at all, merely shaking their heads or smiling. In the Senate of the United States, on the other hand, a man has been able to take the floor and speak for longer than twenty-four hours, in the achievement of what is known as the filibuster, a time-taking device intended to obstruct the voting on a measure.

The young American said, "Suppose you were about to be executed and you were asked that question, what would you say?"

"Fuck you. What else?"

"But you were saying you felt somebody might have made a prolonged reply, and I thought you meant that if it were you, you would make such a reply."

"Perhaps I might, but it isn't too likely, as I am impatient by nature. My whole family has always been impatient. We had a man a couple of hundred years ago who was greeted in the street one morning by a man he despised, to whom he said, 'Who are you to greet me?' And he put a sword through the man, was tried, and taken to be hung, but the scaffolding had not yet been built and the carpenters were busy hammering it together. He was asked if he had anything to say, and he said, 'Yes. Stop that stupid hammering.' Now, of course, you understand this is only a story, a little of the lore of an imaginative family, but there is enough truth in it to have kept it alive for so long. My son knows it, and is amused and comforted by it, since he also is impatient. If a man is about to be hung, he isn't likely to want to postpone the event, unless he believes he can postpone it forever: that is to say, unless he believes there is a plot among his friends to rescue him, and it is only that they appear to be a little late. That has happened, I believe. At any rate, I saw it as a kid at the movies two or three times, and read about it in a number of novels. If I was about to be hung, and I was asked that question, and I had reason to believe there was a plan to set me free, and the plan was a little delayed and I would soon see the plan in execution, then of course I would begin a prolonged reply to the question."

"What would you say?"

"Well, that doesn't matter very much, actually, although the tone of voice does. I would use a courteous and possibly respectful tone of voice, because people who are hanging somebody like to feel they deserve to be respected. This isn't something they really enjoy doing, they like to feel. It is something they *must* do. A respectful tone of voice is basic. It is used all the time by all sorts of victims in relation to those who are victimizing them. It is a good part of one of the ways to survive at all."

The young American said, "And then suppose after five minutes, or even after ten minutes, the plot to free you did not reveal itself, what then?"

"Well, it all depends, of course. Nobody likes the idea of having been respectful uselessly, nobody can go on forever being clever, not even if his life is at stake. At the same time nobody is willing to suspend belief in the miraculous, in the devotion of his friends, in right, and thus I might find it possible to go on in the same manner a little longer, another five minutes, or another ten."

"Suppose somebody calls out rudely, 'All right, lay off the double talk, and make it snappy.' What would you say?"

"I *am* making it snappy, as God is my witness."

"God?"

"Of course. When you're being clever, or trying to be, you don't go halfway, you go all the way. It's easy to drag God into anything. Anybody can do it, and everybody has. It's easy, also, to be absolutely insincere in an unmistakably sincere way. This also is done all the time, by everybody. Nobody needs to search his soul at that time for the probable truth. Anything that will do is enough, anything that works is the truth. How can any man who is about to be hung know for sure that he is not absolutely sincere? What's the difference, at a time like that?"

"But suppose you *are* guilty, and know it?"

"That doesn't change anything at all, for many reasons. First, nobody is not guilty, or at any rate everybody is guilty enough, so why should I be hung and not somebody else, or, more accurately, everybody else? If you hang one guilty man, don't you have to hang all guilty men, and aren't all men equally guilty? That is to say, equally innocent, if you prefer it that way. Of course they are. Second, the guilty man who is captured is rendered innocent by that very event. Capture absolves guilt, the same as birth itself does. Being tried and condemned *continues* to absolve guilt and to increase innocence. No condemned man lies when he says he is innocent. He is. What else could he possibly be? Neither guilt nor innocence are constants. They are parts of the same thing, being alive and who you are, and not knowing anything worth anything about either. Guilt and innocence succeed one another continuously from the beginning to the end. If it is a form of guilt to be born, it is also a form of innocence. To be born is to be captured and condemned within yourself, and so it is to die, too."

"But suppose you have committed a monstrous crime?"

"That, also, does not change anything. Whose crime, for instance, is more monstrous, the man who kills with a knife or the man who founds a gospel? Is the bad man the criminal, or is the good man who doesn't keep his goodness to himself? The first kills one man, the second *impels* the killing of many. Both kill in the heat of emotion, and emotion is always swift, and hardly ever not at least a little correctible, at least a little inaccurate. All emotion is very close to crime, if we are willing to speak of crime at all, if we are willing to agree at the outset that we are using a word that is very nearly meaningless. Isn't it a crime, for instance, not to keep your own emotionality, your own confusion, to yourself?"

The young American finished his third cup of coffee and said he would come back on Friday at three o'clock in the afternoon with a tape-recorder and a list of written questions, if that was all right with me. I said it was fine, I would be ready.

CHAPTER NINETEEN

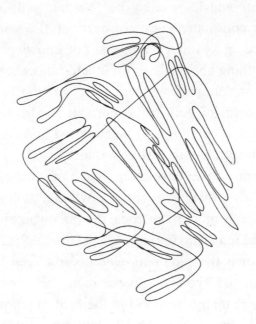

On Friday I was ready, but again the young man wasn't. He didn't show up, and he didn't telephone. Well, that was all right. Anything I had to say would keep.

Now, when my son arrived in Paris he said he wanted to use up the summer going after three things: drawing, writing, and music. He wanted to make a lot of drawings, or, rather, to continue to do so. He had hit upon a kind of nonrepresentational drawing a long time ago, on his visits to my house on the beach at Malibu. He had tossed them into the wastebasket and I had fished them out and kept them. He had also done a little writing, working very slowly, though, because he didn't know how to write on the typewriter, and wasn't free or swift in his handwriting. All the same, the stuff he wrote had clarity and intelligence, and now and then real insight. He enjoyed reading a wide variety of writers, but he didn't seem to have any impulse to write fiction or poetry. He wrote what I must call science, by which I mean that he wrote about *things:* his drawings, for instance. Now and then, though, he confessed with considerable shyness that he hoped to write fiction and poetry some day. He found a number of my own stories so amazing that he said, "How did you ever happen to write like that? I mean, it's different from any other writing I know, and different from most of your own other writing, too."

I told him that writing happens if a writer keeps after his work. I told him I had found it in order long ago to remind myself frequently that it is necessary always to keep after the whole business of writing, to try for more, for different results by different means.

"A writer is likely to make a fool of himself by trying for more, but I think it's worth it, and I haven't been afraid of making a fool of myself. You can't avoid making a fool of yourself to some extent in any case, no matter what you write, or how you write it. If you're afraid of that, you'd better think twice about wanting to be a writer. You can't be bothered about picayune things like seeming to be a fool to other people, or like actually being one, if you want to be a maker of things who doesn't

169

want to become only so skilled that everything he makes is absolutely safe, no harm, no trouble at all, very skilled, very polished, and not much better than another glazed plate to put with a hundred earlier ones of the same kind."

As for the music, his history in that area is quite simple: he has never lived in a house in which there hasn't been a pianola. He has always enjoyed listening to the pianola in operation, to the most famous and popular rolls of forty years ago, which are the only kind I collect and enjoy. At the same time he has heard his mother playing the few pieces she remembers from the time she took lessons, and he has heard me playing the few pieces I invented when I was ten or eleven, which I have continued to play over the years. It followed that he would sooner or later sit at the piano and play. Two years ago he began to play stuff that had a lot of form, progression, and style. These improvisations were sometimes prolonged for half an hour or more, so one evening I set up a tape-recorder near the piano and told him to go ahead, I wanted to get the stuff on tape and play it back. He sat down and moved directly into a brand-new theme, worked it out, kept after it, brought in secondary themes, mingled them all together, and carried everything to an appropriate conclusion, which I was very pleased to notice was not noisy, but clean, clear, unhurried, earnest, simple, and satisfying. I worked the recording machine so that the playing might be heard again from the beginning, and he sat down at the table and listened to what he had just finished making. After he had heard the whole thing he waited a moment, and then he said, "Do you like it?"

I told him I did.

He got up and jigged, which he has been doing most of his life whenever he feels pleased about something, or about himself, and he broke into the pompous, falsetto voice both he and I use when we are kidding ourselves, and he said, "Hey, maybe I'm another Van Heflin."

"Van Cliburn?"

"Nah, I want to be a movie star, because you get all those beautiful girls."

He sat down again and said, "Maybe I ought to take lessons."

I said, "It's too late. Lessons will stop you from playing the way you have had to play from not knowing any better. You might study composition, though, some day."

We let it go at that. Everybody is always letting a lot go at that. There just isn't time to do everything you want to do. I had always wanted to be able to speak through the piano, but I had never been able to get past the few little inventions I had made, which I learned to do in a dozen different ways. This helped me to suspect how much more can always be done in writing.

Well, there was no piano in the Paris apartment, so that left drawing and writing. He went to art galleries every morning, and he made drawings every afternoon and evening. In the meantime, the apartment began to fill up with new books, many of them about art, and new

171

magazines, including the *Paris Review,* a magazine he had been looking at in New York for some time.

One day while we were walking we came to Rue Vernet and when we reached Number Sixteen I said, "Upstairs there is the *Paris Review.*"

We stopped a moment to study the doorway, and then I remembered the young American who had visited me at the George V Hotel, and I thought it might be interesting to go upstairs and meet whoever might be in the office, so my son and I went upstairs, but everybody had gone to lunch. It was a good little editorial office, and my son liked the looks of it very much.

When we were back in the street he said, "I'd like to be in that magazine. I'm going to write something about six or seven of my best drawings and mail them to them."

I told him to take them up and to meet the editors. For three or four days he made new drawings, and one afternoon he wrote a one-page piece about the six or seven he had decided to offer to the editors. He asked me to look at the drawings he had chosen and to read what he had written about them. He had gotten a little excited about this project and he had taken to biting his fingernails again—after having stopped entirely for longer than a week.

I said, "I see you're biting them again."

"Yeah," he said, laughing, "I guess I can't help being worried about what the editors are going to think of this stuff."

"Well, don't be, because it's good stuff, both the drawings and the writing, and not because you happen to be fifteen years old, either. That's not too young, by any means. Bite your fingernails all you've got to, that doesn't matter at all, but it isn't necessary to worry, and I ought to know."

"Well, when you sent out your first stories, you worried, didn't you?"

"I still do, but that doesn't mean it's necessary at all."

"I can't help it, that's all. Boy, if I make the *Paris Review!*" And I knew the jig and the falsetto voice were next: "Fifteen years old, and a millionaire." And then he was off on his famous parody of American success: "Boys, if you want to do something, don't talk about it, do it, that's all. My father said I was a fool, but I showed him, I didn't argue with him, I did my work. I didn't think about it and talk about it, I did it, and you've got to do the same, boys, if you want to be famous and rich, the way I am."

Well, he does it to make me laugh, and I *do* laugh, because he does it so well, and because I know he is doing it to break it up a little, break up the pressure of expectation, get back to size, to the facts, as the saying is, to reality. He knows a lot of talented people who just haven't been able to make a name for themselves, and this troubles him, because he doesn't want that to happen to him.

"Why aren't they famous?"

"Who knows? Something's missing, I guess."

"What is this thing?"

"Well, it's hard to say, but when a man *is* something in himself, others soon know it."

"Like Giacometti?"

"Precisely."

A painter had taken me one night to Giacometti's table in one of the famous places of the Left Bank, and all Giacometti had done during the half-hour in which the painter had tried to engage him in conversation was bark, *"Como?"* I hadn't known who Giacometti was, but I had told my son he was himself entirely and unmistakably: the way he sat, the way he looked at whoever was near, the way he tried to listen, and the way he barked *"Como?"*

My son told me who Giacometti was, and the next day he took me to an art gallery and showed me some of Giacometti's sculpture.

After my son had jigged and laughed at himself, at me as well, he gathered his drawings and his piece about them together and asked for an envelope to put them in. And after he had put them in the envelope he invited me to walk to the Post Office with him, to mail them. I told him not to mail them, to take them up himself. The anxiety came back stronger than ever. He really didn't want to do that, so he said, "Well, on Monday, then."

On Monday we walked to 16 Rue Vernet, but all of a sudden he didn't want to take the stuff up.

Suddenly, though, after we had walked half a block past the entrance he said, "The hell with this. I'm going up there."

His sister said, "They'll laugh at you."

She likes to give him a bad time, but he knows she is really his friend, in all probability his best friend in the whole world. Her opinion seems to mean more to him than the opinion of anybody else, at any rate.

Now, though, he gave her a dirty look, and then he said, "That's what you think."

And he took off.

He was back in three minutes. "There was nobody up there again, they're always out to lunch, so I scribbled a note and clipped it to the envelope, and left it on the table."

For three days he waited for one of the editors to telephone, biting his fingernails all the time, so one day on our way to the Champs-Elysées I guided the walk to Rue Vernet, and when we came to Number Sixteen, he stopped, recognizing the place suddenly, and he looked at his watch.

The time was almost one o'clock and he said, "They're probably out to lunch again."

His sister said, "Is that so? Then, who is that at the window?"

He looked up and said, "That's probably Nelson W. Aldrich, Jr., the Paris Editor."

His sister dared him to go up and find out if the editor wanted his drawings and his piece about them.

"Nah," he said, "I ought to give them time." But after a moment he said, "Well, maybe I ought to find out if they've even had time to look at the stuff."

By that time we were walking away, and he stopped suddenly, and this time he took off at a trot.

My daughter said, "You shouldn't encourage him to think he can get in a magazine that runs drawings by guys like Chagall and all sorts of other world-famous artists. He's going to feel awfully hurt when they don't want his stuff, which is no good, really, and you know it."

"His stuff *is* good, and I *do* know it, and they would be fools not to use it. I'm not saying they *are* going to use it, I'm saying they're fools if they don't."

We began to walk on, but soon we heard him. We turned, and we saw that he was carrying the brown Manila envelope, and smiling.

"Ha ha," his sister laughed. "They didn't want your stuff."

"That's right. I'm glad I went up, though."

We walked on in silence, and then all of a sudden we began to talk about the whole thing.

CHAPTER TWENTY

The young American never came around with the tape-
recorder, and so there was no interview for the *Paris
Review*. Before my son's drawings were rejected by one
of the editors, I had thought of having my son ask the
questions.

"Sure, Pop, I'll ask all the questions you like."

But after the editor had rejected my son's stuff I said,
"O.K., just for that I won't give that lousy magazine an
interview."

And my son, still angry and hurt, said, "Ah, no, that

would be silly. Just because they didn't want my stuff doesn't mean that you have got to keep yourself out of the magazine, out of that series, *The Art of Fiction*. You *ought* to be in it."

"Don't let this little rejection bother you. It has very little to do with the drawings themselves, or with your writing. There are going to be a lot of other rejections the rest of your life, and of course these rejections have got to start somewhere, and you have got to know how they affect you, and you have got to learn how to put up with them, so at least you have made a beginning. You and I will do the interview some day, but it won't be for the *Paris Review*. We'll send it to another magazine."

By taxi we went out to a place called Maisons-Laffitte in time to see the finish of the first race. And then we drank Cokes and wandered over the lawns to where the horses for the next race were being led around by small boys. It was great out there, and we didn't care about the *Paris Review,* all we cared about was being out there under the horse-chestnut trees, and then at the railing to watch the jockeys and the horses fighting for first place in the stretch, as the people shouted their desperate wishes, and we shouted ours. All we cared about was being alive on a hot Sunday afternoon in Paris that year, that month, that day. We jumped over the flower beds to reach a patch of lawn under the shade of a great horse-chestnut tree before somebody else reached it, and a constellation of dancing black spots swarmed about my head, and I said, "Christ, I haven't jumped in years. It's a shock to my fat old body. We got the winner in the second race, who do you like in the third?"

And that was us, that was the day we were there, alive, unkillable, and very nearly as true as any of us is ever permitted to be. It didn't matter that we had bet only a thousand francs each on the winner, the smallest bet we had ever made, for we had agreed to begin slowly, and to see about guessing right every time, for we have no illusions about the horses, the jockeys, the owners, the trainers, the races, or any of the rest of it. We knew it is always no more than guessing, and all we were concerned about was to see if we might guess right. We had done it first crack out of the box, and it is easy to do when you do it. It makes you think the good messages are coming at last, straight from the horse's mouth, as the saying is. And it isn't the money, it isn't that at all, it's the marvel of it. Ten horses in a race, and there at the wire is your own horse, the one you decided was going to do it. We shook hands on it. We had a winning day, each of us, and on our way home my son wanted to ask a lot of questions, which he likes to do on all of our long taxi rides.

"Why did Eugene O'Neill write that letter to his son Shane?"

That was the question that started it.

"Well, there's no telling, of course."

That was the answer, or, rather, the beginning of the first answer.

Working with Shane O'Neill, now a grown man with a wife and kids of his own, somebody had written a book

179

about Eugene O'Neill, and one of the big weekly magazines had run a condensed version of the book. I had read the stuff and I had studied the photographs, and then my son had, too, and a long time afterwards he had suddenly asked about the letter.

"O'Neill appears to have been unhappy about what he was doing at that time, to begin with. He was abandoning his wife and his kids, and he was going off with a younger woman, a rather dazzling one. He was famous, he was still a young man, and he was willing to turn his back on his marriage, his wife, and his kids. At the same time he probably felt deeply guilty about this, and doubtful about his own future in this new arrangement, with this new woman. He certainly had no children with her, as it turned out, and near the end of his life he accused her of being mad, and she accused him of the same thing. It may be that he had *wanted* things to turn out that way for him. Shane was a small boy, and of course O'Neill had been a small boy at one time, too. The impression I got was that in writing to Shane he became Shane without ceasing to be O'Neill. The letter was more to himself when he had been Shane's age than to Shane, who was of course somebody else again entirely. There is a hint of disaster in it that is at least premature. It was as if he were instructing his son to fail, not so much in the achievement of anything in particular, but to fail at the outset in all of it, in any aspect of it, as if he were telling him that he didn't really have a chance against disorder, drunkenness, disease, death itself—because here was his own

180

father in the midst of all these things, saying he doubted if he and his son would ever meet again. Why wouldn't they meet again if O'Neill wanted them to meet again? As it happens, they did meet again, many times, but the damage may be said to have been done—or the good, for you must know that bad things, the very worst things, can and frequently do affect somebody in a good way, while good things, the best things, can affect somebody else in a very bad way. We just don't know how anything is likely to affect anybody. I am willing to believe that O'Neill was willing to send the letter to his son in the belief that it might do the boy good. Otherwise, there is no accounting for it."

My son said, "Listen, Pop, that letter couldn't do any boy any good at all. Do you know, I cried when I read it?"

"Well, of course, that isn't hard to believe or to understand. After all, your own father and mother separated while you were still a small boy, and you know something about what a thing like that does to a man, what it did to you, and I don't. I can guess, but that's all, and my guess isn't likely to be a very good one. My father, for instance, was dead and gone before I so much as knew him, at all. I had only one small, insignificant memory of him, and it was a dismal one at that. And then he died, which of course I had no way of understanding at the time, since I wasn't even three years old. But his death never seemed to me to be a betrayal of me, as in a sense it was, for a father has simply got to keep himself alive until his kids are grown enough to accept or reject him as he is, or to do both, as needed, by turns. In sleep we understand these things a little better than we do when we are awake, but I don't remember ever having said to my father in sleep, 'How dare you abandon me?' And I *did* meet him in sleep, or at any rate I did now and then meet somebody I believed was him, which is the same thing, most likely, and I did speak to him. I know I never raged against him. I can't pretend that I remember accurately anything I said to him in sleep, but I know it was all in the nature of a statement of *rightness,* of well-being, of plans, but especially of one plan in particular, not unlike what I had come to believe had been his own plan, in which he had failed: that is, to write. If I may be permitted to guess what I might have actually said to him in sleep at one time or another, I suppose it might be said to have been something like, 'Well, I have made up my mind to write, and I believe I shall.' Well, why should my father's early death have had that effect on me instead of another? Who knows? Every man is a mystery. There is no use expecting to be able to measure this mystery, or to account for it. Until I myself had become a father it had been inconceivable to me that my father in dying had done an absurd thing, a foolish thing, an unfair and unnecessary thing, but after I had become a father, after I had reached almost as many years of time as he had reached in all of his life, I began to believe that he had died because he had permitted himself to die, and I was not unwilling to be annoyed with such weakness, not on my account, but on his. Now, I must make known to you that there is a very powerful and yet not entirely accountable order of sorrow in my family, which is surely in yourself, too, which you must recognize, accept, understand, and seek to control, for this sorrow, while not entirely useless, can be deeply troublesome, and in the end actually killing. Everybody has it, most likely, in one degree or another, but my family has it excessively. In the old days this kind of constant sorrow was called melancholy, or melancholia, and anybody who had it was said to be neurasthenic. Nowadays it is the style to say the man has a powerful death wish. Well, a father just hasn't got the right not to kick out the death wish. He has got to kick it out, he has got to stay alive, he has got to work at it, he has got to fight it out until he is an old man, and then if he feels like it, at the age of eighty-eight, for instance, he can give over to it, and die. His kids are themselves old by that time, too, and their kids are well along, and have little kids of their own, so it is all right to let the death wish prevail. If it isn't easy to be a son, it isn't easy to be a father, either, and most of us just don't ever quite make it. That's our story."

When we got home my daughter had baked a cake, this time with shortening, which she had left out of the cake she had baked the day before, because she hadn't known that shortening is butter, as she said, and she had made a salad, and had set the table, waiting for my son to make hamburgers, and finally she had finished reading *The Scarlet Letter* by Nathaniel Hawthorne, a book

I have never read, a book she is required by her school to read during the summer, along with six or seven others. She had wept at the end of the book, and it was obvious that the reading of it had affected her deeply. She was hushed and glad, and that's pretty good going for any book, so I decided to have a look at the book at the first opportunity. I had always imagined that the letter was an epistle, but my daughter let me know that it isn't at all, it is the letter A, for Adultery.

After supper, after a long walk in the hot but pleasant evening, along the tree-shaded streets of our neighborhood, and the broad boulevards farther off, she brought me the book and showed me what she had written on the inside of the back cover: "I have just finished reading this book, The Scarlet Letter, and be it of any interest to the next person who ventures to read it I personally *aclaim* it a heartbreaking work of art, written by a master of perfection, *Nathanael* Hawthorne. On this date of July 26, 1959, I have closed this book with a tear of sheer marvel in my eye, which I am sure will be shared by any fortunate person who perchance is the next to read The Scarlet Letter."

And then, after I had read the foregoing aloud, she said, "I used words like *perchance* and *be it of any interest* because that's the way he writes, but it really is a wonderful book."

"I had no idea, but now I'm sure, and I'm going to read it, or at least read around in it, very soon. What you have written shows the power of one writer over another, and even though your usage of his style isn't quite flawless—you've misspelled one word and his first name, for instance—it gives me a pretty good idea of what his style is like—ornamental, that is."

Well, for an hour or more the three of us played freeze-out stud, using matches for chips, and risking five hundred francs apiece, which is the equivalent of a dollar. I was the first to go, and after quite a struggle my son won all of the matches from my daughter and five hundred francs from each of us, which of course pleased him very much.

Well, here they are the following day, sorry to be intruding, the boy to complain about another fight with the woman in the kitchen, about the refrigerator this time, the girl to complain about her brother's complaining, which she feels is unnecessary and out of order. And so I have got to get up from my worktable and consider the matter. My son turned the cold dial of the refrigerator from three to seven, whereupon the poor woman charged at him and at the refrigerator, and turned it back to three, screaming as she always does, and making painful faces as she always does: "No, no." And then she screamed the name of the man from whom I am renting this apartment, meaning that he had given her instructions not to move the dial past three. My son said he didn't care what the man's instructions to her might be, he wanted the refrigerator to be cold, so his Cokes would *become* cold. He said he was living in the house now, and then the woman came right back and said that she was in the house on behalf of the landlord.

My daughter said, "He has a fight with her every morning, and it's his own fault. Something's the matter with the refrigerator, that's all. Something's the matter with the stove, too, and we know the toilet in the big bathroom has never worked, not even after the plumber had been up here six times, and had taken the water tank away for almost a week. But what's the use fighting *her?* She's just a poor woman who has been made into a slave by rich people, and she's going home to Yugoslavia with her small son for a month in only six more days. I've gone out of my way to be especially nice to her for a whole week, and I don't care if she isn't nice to me, because I know she doesn't know any better."

My son listened to all this, and then he said, "Is she a watchdog for these lousy people who push her around, or what? I thought she was supposed to work for us, but all she does is scream no, no, and make faces. I want my Cokes to be cold, that's all."

The fact is the poor woman is lost among people who do not order her around politely, as the woman of the house does, or with anger, as the man of the house does. All is right in the world as long as she feels she is serving her superiors, but just let anybody come along who doesn't want anybody to be either superior or inferior, and her understanding is shot to hell.

My son has had a long history of bitter fights with a whole mob of demented women who have come into his life one by one. He just can't tolerate the breed. They bug him, as he says.

Last night I picked up Hawthorne's book to see what he had to say, beginning with the author's preface to the second edition: which was a recitation of his reasons for not changing one word in his Introduction to the first edition, which appears to have displeased certain people. And then I began to read the Introduction itself: "It is a little remarkable, that—though disinclined to talk over-much of myself and my affairs at the fireside, and to my personal friends—an autobiographical impulse should twice in my life have taken possession of me, in addressing the public. The first time was three or four years since, when I favored the reader—inexcusably, and for no earthly reason, that either the indulgent reader or the intrusive author could imagine—with a description of my way of life in the deep quietude of an Old Manse. And now—because, beyond my deserts, I was happy enough to find a listener or two on the former occasion—I again seize the public by the button, and talk of my three years' experience in a Custom House."

Well, now, how old was he when he wrote *that?* Surely not much more than thirty seven, my father's age when he died, but at least Hawthorne was still alive at the time, and with his kids, if he had any. I must one day soon buy a good biography of him. Did Edmund Wilson do one, or, rather, since I know he didn't, I wish he had, because he knows how to do them better than anybody else I can think of, and I'd like to know what he makes of this writer. Apart from the fact that his writing is unnecessarily laden over with the lard of language, and is consequently oily and slippery, he speaks of something or other he calls the public on the one hand, and of somebody called the author on the other, as if the first were in fact a real body, a group with a single identity, a multitude, and not one man at a time, and as if the second, the author, were in hiding, and properly so, since if he came out of hiding the public would be shocked by the sight of him, either because he was so unlike the public, or so unlike any member of the public, and so must not be seen, except in the little appearances he might perchance, as my daughter would say, make in his stories. It is a very long introduction and I won't pretend that I was able to put up with very much of it, although I am willing to believe that a time may come when I will be able to read every word of it.

My daughter needed six or seven days of painful reading to finish the Introduction alone, and three or four more to get into the heart of the story itself, but yesterday suddenly she was able to rush through all that remained to be read. Hawthorne is surely no slob, and he used a kind of language, a kind of style, that may have been very nearly inevitable in his day—for a gentleman, but why in God's name should a gentleman mess around with writing at all? Gentlemen should please ladies, and let it go at that, shouldn't they? And at the end of the book, a paperback that sells for thirty-five cents, I read the Afterword by Maxwell Geismar. And this is how it starts: "The literary revival of the middle of the last century saw the publication of *The Scarlet Letter* in 1850, *Moby Dick* in 1851, and *Leaves of Grass* in 1855. These three great books were the primary documents, and the monuments, of what we might call the Puritan underground." And later: "Hawthorne kept the human drama moving by the use of multiple levels of action and reflection. (Notice the changing symbolism of the scarlet A itself.)"

CHAPTER TWENTY-ONE

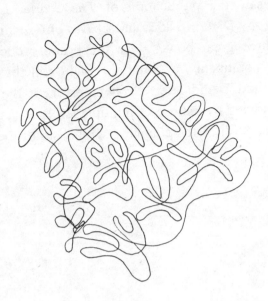

My son said, "Did you read in the Stravinsky book what Gertrude Stein said when somebody asked her why she liked Picasso's paintings? She said, 'I like to look at them.' How about that?"

"An excellent example of summing up."

"And what about Picasso himself, talking about Matisse? He said Matisse was a bowl of flowers on a table. Why did Picasso say an insulting thing like that?"

"Well, it was long ago, they were both young, they hadn't found out who they were, it was the proper time for arrogance and insults."

"But isn't Picasso still insulting others, especially other painters?"

"Picasso moves ahead. With him it is *always* a thrust, his restlessness is incurable, he cannot rest, his work does not seek repose, as the work of a number of other older painters does, he remains young, he has got to insult somebody."

"We've got almost an hour in this taxi before we reach Tremblay. Let's do an interview for the *Paris Review*."

"O.K."

"Well, to begin with, who are you? Who do you think you are? Who were you? Who do you think you would like to become?"

"Oh ho, what are you trying to do, make it impossible for me to answer at all? I don't know who I am, I don't know who I think I was, I don't know who I was, who I have been, but I know I would like to become who I am, if you can understand that. And I'm sure you can guess the reason why. I have no choice. Ask me another, then."

"Why do you write?"

"I write because writing is my work, and it is better for me to work than it is for me not to work, although I have always hoped for the time when I would discover that it is better for me not to work than it is for me to work."

"Why?"

"I have always had a sneaking suspicion that work is a kind of excuse for failure, general failure—to know, to understand, to cherish, to love, to believe, and so on. It is a kind of evasion, a kind of escape from the knowledge that one is entirely without grace, that one is altogether ill and mad."

"If you could stop working, what would you do instead?"

"That's the trouble. What could I possibly do? The same things, most likely. In the morning I would get up. At night I would go to sleep. I would walk, I suppose. I *have* longed to walk for a whole year, for instance. I once believed the time had come for me to take off on a walk across the American continent, from San Francisco to New York, but I got drunk instead, and the next day I wrote a short story. That was before I had become a published writer, I may say, and one of the reasons I didn't start walking was that all I had to my name was one silver dollar that I had won at petty gambling the day before."

"How many dollars did you believe you ought to have in order to start walking?"

"Two. Besides, I had only one pair of shoes at the time, and they were already shot. I didn't think I ought walk in my bare feet."

"What else do you think you might do if you could find out how to stop working?"

"I would write, I guess."

"But that's work, that's your *only* work."

"I know, but what I'm trying to say is that I would write in a way that was no longer work."

"Is there such a way?"

"There may be. As it is, one of the reasons I can't stop working is that the only way I know how to earn a living is to write, and if you expect to get something for what you write, writing is work."

"Something? Or just plain money? Which?"

"Well, money, but then there's no getting away from the truth that money is entangled in everything. In getting something better than money, in trying to get it, it turns out that you get money, too. Pretty soon there is nothing you can try for that isn't at least *likely* to get money, too. You spoke of Gertrude Stein a moment ago. She tried for something, but it didn't seem to be anything that might bring her money, and then all of a sudden it did."

"Did that change what she had tried for?"

"Of course it did. She liked the idea, I suppose. And she liked the idea of being famous, too. Money and fame affect what you have done, what you are doing, and what you are going to do."

"What can you try for in writing that is better than fame and money?"

"To do something worth doing insofar as you can seize upon a theory of worth that seems valid for you."

"In writing, then, what's worth doing?"

"Well, it has a way of always turning out that very nearly anything you did was worth doing, but now and then it turns out that what you did *was* actually something, a little more than you had expected, but you have always got to take a chance in the first place."

"Yes, but what is the nature of this something? Do you

mean the thing written is easy to read, or that it says something, or that it does something to the reader, or what? Can't anything be pinned down?"

"Not really. The something is probably only a belief you have about what you have done. 'This is O.K.,' for instance. 'This is better than anything else I have done,' for instance. 'This may not be better than anything else anybody else has ever done, most likely, but it *is* a good thing in itself to begin with, and then it is also a good thing in relation to all of the other good things.' And so on."

"Well, what is a good thing, then?"

"A drink of cold water is a good thing when you're thirsty."

"Of course, but what is a good thing in writing?"

"Well, we could talk forever and not really reach a conclusion, but that's all right, too. We talk forever, in any case, and it is only a question of what we talk about. In writing, a good thing is a thing that has movement that seems natural and inevitable, a kind of motion that can't be arrested. It's always there, waiting for somebody to read and to be moved by the movement."

"Why else do you write?"

"I began, as most writers do, in the expectation of changing the world. It *is* chaos, as you know, and a kid just can't cherish chaos. He wants order. He wants balance. He wants rightness. I also meant to change the nature or pose of man, of the human race."

"Well, did you? I mean, even a little?"

194

"Who knows?"

"Insofar as I am the human race, I did."

"For the better?"

"Don't you?"

"I mean, who knows how else he might have changed had he chosen to work on a vineyard instead of at a table, writing? My writing after I had written it probably changed me for the better, and to that extent it might also have changed the human race for the better, but the best change in me happened *while* I was writing my writing. It happened because I sat there and tried to make something. I used to believe my face was coarse, for instance, but after I had finished writing something, I noticed that my face was suddenly no longer coarse. The work had changed me so powerfully inside that you could see it in my face, which was still the same face, but no longer coarse. I gave this a lot of thought after I first noticed it. When you work at the making of a new piece of writing you gradually put away from yourself a lot of trash that is in your nature. You concentrate so intensely that in a sense you leave your body entirely, although it's there all the time. Your spirit, or *the* spirit, takes over—not for long, the spirit doesn't need a lot of time, it certainly doesn't need forever. It operates entirely in the instant, now, canceling time as we understand it. Afterwards, a writer notices that he has worked three hours, for instance, or perhaps only thirty minutes, but now and then six or seven hours, which he hadn't noticed as minutes or hours, or as time at all. The work of writing, of trying to write, made the change, not the writing, after it was written. Well, work is work, and if one order of work changes a man for the better, it is likely that another order does, too. If I had worked on a vineyard from the time I was sixteen, I'm not sure I might not have changed for the better again. I didn't, however, and that's the end of the matter. We get a view of the condition of the human spirit in the human face, especially in the eyes. The human spirit as revealed by the face and the eyes seems to be most alive in the two extremes of men: the simplest and the most complex, the least developed and the most. In between, you see very little of the human spirit, if you see any of it at all. This suggests there is something the matter with the work most people do."

"What *is* the matter with it?"

"I don't really know, of course, although I suspect that even more than writing, for instance, and even more than looking after a vineyard, the work by which most people earn a living is nothing in itself, nothing more than the using up of a certain amount of time of so many days of the week, an order of usage that does not impel the spirit to take over, and on the contrary probably drives the spirit farther and farther afield, so to say."

"Then, you do not feel that your own writing, for instance, after twenty-five years, has changed the world or the human race?"

"Only insofar as it has changed me, as I've said. But that may not be as bad as it sounds, for if my work hasn't changed the world and its inhabitants for the better, it

196

also hasn't changed them for the worse. I chose writing as my profession, as the means by which I would earn my way, by which I would keep myself in a position to keep after everything, because I knew of no other work that was less likely to change anything or anybody for the worse. If my writing couldn't help, I didn't see how it might hinder, although of course even that is a theory, since a great deal of writing has changed man and the world for the worst."

"Do you mean bad writing?"

"I do, of course, but I also mean a lot of writing which if it cannot be called good is certainly effective."

"What *is* good writing?"

"Well, there we are again, back where it isn't easy to make a reply that isn't bound to be general and therefore inaccurate. Good writing is writing done by a good man."

"Just like that? And of course you mean *you* are a good man, don't you?"

"I mean I *try,* I suppose."

"You drink and gamble and keep bad hours and all that stuff, and you aren't a very good friend, you don't really have any friends at all, according to what I've heard. You speak in the loudest voice I've ever heard. You dominate every group I've ever seen you in. You almost never seem interested in anybody else, unless it's an attractive woman. You're very swift and rude with people you don't like. You're self-centered, arrogant, vain, vulgar, and really very ignorant—you know less

197

about the details of what's going on in the world, for instance, than even I do, and you don't care about that, either, you don't think that that is any reason why you can't explain everything to everybody, including experts. You make people nervous and uncomfortable just by being among them. You're always clearing your throat and spitting if you're in the street, or burying the stuff in a handkerchief if you're indoors. And a lot more. So how can you believe you are a good man?"

"Have you got the idea that it is necessary to be dead in order to be good? I can't deny any of the charges you've made, but why should that make me believe I'm not a good man? I've got to be who I am, don't I? If I stopped being who I am and thereby gave an *appearance* of being good, would I actually be anything at all? Within the framework of who I am, I find it both possible and inevitable to believe I am a good man, and as writing is my work I find it possible to believe that my writing, whenever it turns out to be good, is good because it was written by a good man."

"Is the book you are now writing, which you will finish writing in a few days, a good book?"

"I don't know. For one thing, it isn't finished yet, and for another I have made a point of not looking at any of it, of not looking back at any of it, which isn't the way I usually work, or the way any writer usually does, as far as I know. But I remember that even when I *did* examine every morning the work of the previous day, or all of the work I had done so far, I never could be sure about the whole work until it was finished, and sometimes not even then. It is always safe, however, to believe the work isn't any good, and, as you know, I haven't liked this work at all. Even so, whenever you have asked me about it and I have replied honestly that I dislike it, I am able to believe it might turn out to be less bad than I imagine, and might in fact, perhaps for its very badness, turn out to be good, for there is something to be said for the bad, too, although I am not prepared at this time to go into detail about that. It is a little too complicated for a man on his way to an afternoon at the races."

"Well, what I don't understand is how you can go right on working from one day to another, Saturdays and Sundays and holidays, on a book you yourself don't like."

"Very simple. To begin with I long ago discovered that it is better to finish a new work than to abandon it, for if a writer isn't careful, if he abandons one new work and then another, he will soon be doing nothing else. The pattern will become established, and he won't be able to finish anything. I also discovered that it is premature to reach a decision about a thing before it *is* a thing, before it's achieved, before it has a reality of its own, apart from the man who wrote it, who insisted on writing it. Premature and useless. Furthermore, I also discovered that while it is a very good thing for a writer to make a good beginning, to start a new work in what appears to be precisely the right place, from whence it must follow that the whole work will move naturally and easily to its proper end, even this isn't absolutely necessary, and if

199

the truth is told, any place is the right place to make a beginning. I keep after this particular book because as you know I must remain in Paris in order to be available at any time, at a moment's notice, to the lawyer who is trying to set up a procedure of working and earning that will permit me to accumulate the money I need for the tax collector. Inasmuch as I knew I had to stay in Paris in any case, I wanted to use up the time in a way that would bring me a new work of some kind, and let it be any kind at all, it would be better than nothing. I would have something to put aside, at any rate. The whole month would be gone suddenly, and there on my table would be a new work. One day I would notice that the whole month had gone by, and I would be pleased to notice that as the month had been going I had managed to make this new thing. There are other reasons too, and they may be as good as any I have named. For instance, I like trying to get two or three things done at the same time. I like working under pressure, too, for I have found that having all the time in the world in which to achieve something doesn't necessarily improve the quality of the thing achieved, and frequently does the opposite. Nobody needs all the time in the world, and nobody can effectively use more than a little of his allotted time in the making of something. Also, as you know, I had just finished the writing of a play—for money, which I needed desperately, because I had gambled and lost. I got the money, which I considered quite an achievement under the circumstances, and the money in turn got me a number of things I especially wanted and need, the first of which was a place to rest, and then the right to rest, since I was at last out of trouble, out of the rate race of gambling and losing. Now, this is the important thing about having a place to rest, and a right to rest: the minute you *have* these things, you find yourself rested. The very fact that you have them rests you, and you are ready to move along to the stuff that must follow rest, whether it is a new work of writing or a new crack at luck, at gambling, and at the theory that this time you can win, this time you are going to win. Although the play was written for money, I am not going to belittle it. If I hadn't written it, if I hadn't been able to write it, and even if I had written it and it hadn't been good enough to *seem* to be worth money, my goose was cooked. Since it wasn't cooked, as it turned out, I was so pleased that I wanted to enjoy my good luck by starting a new work, without suspending, at least entirely, any of the other necessary or desirable activities of my life. Thus, I started writing the book."

"What's it about?"

"About not dying, to begin with. And after that it's about a man being a father, about having been a son, about time, about art, about talk."

"You mean it's about yourself, don't you?"

"Of course, but anything any writer writes is about himself. And I began to write the book so that the writing of it would take the place of dying, of my own literal death, which I had been feeling for some time was near.

201

And I kept writing it as if the writer had long since disappeared from among the living. My spiritual health was shot when I began to write, if in fact my physical health wasn't, too, as it certainly seemed to be, and of course a man perishes in the failure of his spiritual health."

"You don't actually mean you think you were dying, do you? Pop, you know you're as strong as a bull."

"A bull dies in the failure of his spiritual health, too, and you yourself know from having seen a number of first-rate bullfights, and from having read a number of first-rate books about them, that in the most effective fight the bull and the matador become one, like a body and a spirit. The bull, virtually bursting with physical health, engages in a mortal struggle with the man, whose physical health is negligible. They are total strangers at the outset, possibly even enemies, but little by little something in each of them is shared, is passed from one to the other in a ritual of trial and error, and in a series of formal exchanges. The Spaniards and all of the others who love bullfights go to them to behold themselves as both the bull and the matador, neither of whom they are able to love unless both of them come to a moment of love, called the moment of truth, out of pride, rage, ignorance, misunderstanding, pain, hatred, respect, and finally humility. A man can be as strong as a bull and still be dying. I don't want this to become mystical or anything like that, but the fact is that every man is a bull and a matador in a mortal struggle in his own bull ring.

And yes, I *do* mean I think I was dying, and I still am. Of course I'm dying. I've always been. It's just that after the passing of fifty years of time through your blood and bone, your sleep and memory, you begin to *know* it as you've never before known it, and that's when you've got to watch it a little bit more than ever before, and differently, too."

"Well, here we are at Tremblay."

"We'll have lunch, and then we'll go out and look at the horses, and then we'll watch them run."

"I want melon and steak, the same as last time."

"I'll go along with that."

CHAPTER TWENTY-TWO

Last Night is a title to which I have for thirty years expected to append a novel, but the poor title has remained
unfulfilled, perhaps because the idea I have, the idea I
have always had, for the fulfilling, is such a difficult one
to achieve: all of the last nights, all experience, all error,
and all truth, brought together in one last night. There
have been a number of other titles of this kind which
have come back to mind, asking again to be fulfilled, but
they have been neglected, too. Still, it is never too late,
most likely, and I still expect some day to write a novel

called *Last Night*. Also, a book called *Yes,* which I know is not a good title, since it can have the effect of quickly annoying anyone who guesses at the probable implications of it, which he is likely to feel are bound to be banal. As a rule a writer does not write to a title. He writes, and after he has written, he *chooses* a title that he believes is right for what he has written. Now and then, though, it happens the other way around: a whole work is almost ready-made in a title, and all the writer needs to do is find the time in which to permit the work to become written.

I woke up from an order of grand sleep I have known only half a dozen times in my life early one morning when I was thirteen or fourteen years of age knowing I had just read, in an instant, a whole long book which was my own, which I had not however written, and for an instant of half-wakefulness I knew every word in the book, and I believed I would be able to get the whole book on paper instantly, whereupon I came to full wakefulness and remembered how slowly writing is put to paper. I remembered the truth about us, and I forgot the book, or, rather, the words of it, a hundred thousand or more of them all in place, and all making a work of wonder. I knew I had had the book, whole and complete, word for word, and while I knew I hadn't actually written it, it *was* mine, and now I had it no longer, nobody had it. I was both pleased that I had had it, that it had come to me, that such a full and total thing could happen at all, and angry that there was not within me, awake, the ability to write out the book, that the pressing upon me of the present made all of the words of it blur and blend and finally disappear, and I could not keep the entirety of the book intact. And I knew that this was essentially the book I would one day write, learn how to write, forgetting how the words had been together, making mistakes, trying to correct them, cheating now and then, whenever there was no other way to keep after the lost assembly and wonder of the words, inventing, lying, and otherwise making do, since it was impossible to get the thing on paper in any other way. We are slow things, and truth is swift, it is instantaneous, it is both always and now, it is complete, and we aren't. Having known the book at all seemed to me to be a confirmation from heaven (or from anything you like, from memory, for instance) that I had been chosen to write it, I had been *commanded* to do so, and I was proud that this was so, even though I knew it was going to be hard work for the rest of my life, no matter how long I might manage to live. I wished I might have the book awake as readily as I had had it asleep, but I knew that that was out of the question. A few words, perhaps, but no more, but when I tried to seize upon even a few words of the book, perhaps the first two or three, or the last, I failed in this, too. The whole thing came in an instant and was gone in an instant, leaving me with the rest of my life to puzzle it out, to seek to write it, to pass it along to somebody else. And I do not mean that a revelation of this sort happens only to a few people. I am sure it happens to everybody. All the same, I was pleased, proud, and puzzled that it had happened to me, for it compelled me to feel chosen, as of course each of us is, in the very event of birth itself.

Well, last night my daughter and my son began to ask me questions, and this morning I want to put to paper what we said. I know this will not extend the book I was commanded so long ago to write, but at the same time I still believe that anything I write is part of that revealed and lost book, the book of my boyhood, of my earliest days as a writer, and that every book I have written contains within it, somewhere, a little of the revealed book.

We had had supper, we had had a pleasant walk after supper, we were home again, the evening was hot and still, we were all in good health, we were comfortable, there was ease and laughter in us, and it was time to talk.

My daughter said, "Who is the greatest man you ever met?"

"I was, but I can't say I ever really met myself, although early one morning as I fell down a flight of stairs in a bar on Market Street in San Francisco, I *almost* did. I was roaring drunk. I was laughing. I had been drinking since early evening with loud friends, and now the time was almost two in the morning. We had wandered from the joints in the North Beach to Market Street, and we had come into this place, which we didn't know. I ordered another drink and asked the bartender where the can was, and he pointed to a door. Well, there were two doors where he pointed, and I was moving swiftly. I wanted to get the hot water out of me, and get back to the bar to my

207

loud friends, for we had been talking all night about art and reality, and we were getting near to the time when we might expect to say something both sensible and amusing. I flung open the first door, stepped in, still laughing, still talking, and began to fall headfirst down a flight of cement stairs. The door swung shut an instant after I knew I was falling, and so I fell in total darkness. Wrong door, I thought, and so instead of being on a level floor, standing happily at the white trough, I'm falling, and this may be it, unless I don't land on my head, in which case I shall certainly be embarrassed. *That* was when I very nearly met myself."

"Did you land on your head?"

"No, I landed on my back, on cement that was wet. I heard no bones break, though. I needed an instant to take inventory, to try to determine the amount of damage, but even while I was in the midst of this taking of inventory, I jumped to my feet, as if by doing this I might prevent some of the inevitable damage, and I was surprised and delighted that I could in fact get up and could stand. Was I hurt? Well, I didn't *seem* to be, and I certainly still needed to get the hot water out of me, so I turned around in the dark and began to climb the stairs. I was sure my friends at the bar would know what had happened and would be amused by it, but when I reached the top of the stairs, pushed the door open, and stepped back into the light, I saw that they were busy with their drinks, their talk, and their own lives. I took the second door this time. No one else was there. I took off my coat and wiped the back of it dry on the roll-towel. I went back to the bar, seized my drink, and swallowed all of it. I told nobody I had taken a fall, and that while I had been falling I had believed I might very well be at the end of my time."

My daughter: "My God, suppose you had landed on your head and died?"

"It would have been awful, because I hadn't yet published one lousy book."

"Who cares about that? What would have happened to me if you had died?"

"Well, your mother would have married somebody else, I suppose, and you would be somebody else, or at least partly somebody else."

"Get a load of him," my son said. "First, he's the greatest man he's ever met, and then he tells his own daughter if he hadn't been her father, somebody else would have."

"Yes, isn't he silly? I couldn't possibly be anybody else."

"So you didn't land on your head, you didn't die, you finally published your first lousy book, and then a hundred and twenty-two others one after another, and so now here you are in Paris, and here we are, too, and all we want to know is who was the greatest man you ever met—outside of yourself, that is."

"Well, I never met anybody who *wasn't* great—on account of the eyes, most likely. I really don't believe it is possible for anybody not to be great, if you want to put it that way instead of the other way. I really don't believe it is possible for anybody not to be insignificant, that is. Everybody shares these two extremes pretty much equally."

"The hell they do. You know there *are* great men."

"It's easy for a great man to be great. It's inevitable—for him, so of course it comes to the same thing. He's just as insignificant as the next fellow, perhaps even more insignificant, since he knows the enormity of his insignificance, while those who aren't great don't, and almost never so much as suspect."

"Who is the greatest man you ever met, period? And no hocus-pocus, please."

"Did you meet Stalin?" my daughter said.

"No, I didn't, but my grandmother, after whom you were named, resembled Stalin to an astonishing degree including in the last years of her life the same kind of mustache, and I certainly met *her*."

My son said, "Your *grandmother* is the greatest man you ever met? Oh boy."

"The fact is she had a lot in common with the Georgian tyrant."

"The hell with your grandmother. I want to know about somebody great outside of your family."

"O.K., then. Mr. Huff."

"Who is Mr. Huff?"

"Mr. Huff was an old popcorn man when I sold papers in Fresno. We shared the Republican Corner for about six months, during which time we became friends. I was nine or ten and he was in his early seventies, I suppose."

"What was great about him?"

"I've written about him somewhere. I spoke about the eyes a moment ago. Well, he had one eye that had been eaten away by a disease of some sort. He wore a piece of thick black cloth over the large cavity where his eye had been. His other eye was watery, bloodshot, sick, and better than half-blind, and yet he pushed the wagon from his furnished room to the corner every day and he stood there for nine or ten hours, fooling around with the machinery in the wagon, making popcorn, and selling it to anybody who wasn't afraid of him, as of course most people were."

"Ah, what was *great* about him?"

"Well, he was my friend."

"That doesn't make him great, does it?"

"It helps. If somebody great notices somebody else, the person noticed acquires greatness, too."

"Oh, no. So you noticed the popcorn man, and therefore he became great?"

"I didn't say that. The fact is the popcorn man noticed *me,* and you know he didn't have a hell of a lot of eyesight to notice me *with.* Yet he did—and rather deeply, too, I might say."

"What did he notice?"

"Well, first of all he noticed that I, like very nearly everybody else in town, was afraid of him. But after a while he began to notice that I wasn't, and then he went and noticed a lot of other stuff."

211

"Such as?"

"Well, I believe he noticed that I had an enormous respect for him, even before we began to speak. We didn't begin, you know, until I had hustled papers on that corner for at least two weeks. I wasn't given to buying popcorn for one thing, and for another he wasn't given to making friends—with anybody. I just minded my own business and he minded his. We understood one another, we acknowledged one another without actually doing so, if you know what I mean, and we let it go at that—at first. I can't remember how it happened that we finally began to talk, but we did."

"So?"

"So we became friends. After school every day I looked forward to seeing him, and I think he looked forward to seeing me. And after six o'clock every evening, after most of the people who worked in the city had gone home, and there was little prospect of either of us making very much money, he would nod to me, by which I understood him to mean I was invited to visit him, and chat, which I was glad to do. He was an atheist, and in his day he had done a lot of reading, and a lot of thinking, too. He wanted me to know what he had read, and what he had decided about the human race, and the meaning of the human experience. He named the writers he had read, and I looked them up at the Public Library, and read them, too, or read around in their most famous books, and we talked—philosophy, for the most part. I thought he was great. I still do."

"O.K., then, Mr. Huff."

"Well," my daughter said, "*you* thought he was great, but nobody else did, and you *must* be willing to admit he wasn't the greatest man you ever met, so who was?"

"He was pretty great, certainly great enough for all practical purposes, and you must bear in mind that this sort of thing has a lot to do with when the meeting happens to take place. My meeting with Mr. Huff took place when it was bound to mean a great deal to me. Like everybody else, he could have taken me for nobody, just another kid in the streets, and so the courtesy of his recognition moved me deeply, and I in turn was impelled to recognize him. He was not simply what he appeared to be, a dirty old man, ugly and diseased. He was in fact a noble and heroic spirit, still standing in proud ruin, asking nothing of God or of man. Of course I have met other great men, but by that time I was great myself, and knew it. Mr. Huff helped me to begin to know it."

"Who *were* the other great men?"

"Well, as you may have gathered by now, I have never permitted myself to impose myself on anybody at all, let alone on somebody who is great. Nowadays anybody who has decided, or, more accurately, half-decided, to become a writer, for instance, or to *think* about it, goes right up to the door of somebody who *is* a writer, to tell him about it. A thing like that, behavior like that, was out of the question for me. I knew there was no help for me as a writer, and nothing for me to learn from any other writer. All I had to do was write, and, writing, find

213

out how to write. There wasn't anything to talk about in this connection at all. If I learned how to write, and if my writing was published, then of course a few people would know about it, including perhaps a few writers, so that if we happened to meet, it wouldn't be necessary for either of us to remark that we were writers, or that we wanted to write, since we *were* writers, and since we *had* written. We could then talk about other things."

"For God's sake, who did you meet?"

"Well, that's the trouble, don't you see? I have in fact met a lot of people, and many of them have enjoyed fame, or at any rate a moment or two of it, but very few of them struck me as being great, in the way you seem to mean."

"You met Shaw, and you know damn well you can't pretend he wasn't great."

"No, I can't. What's more, I liked him, which is another thing entirely. I felt he was far greater than he knew, which I told him, and far greater, even, than he had been able to make known through his plays, prefaces, and public performances, for you must understand that he *was* a performer, or at any rate had chosen for some reason to pretend that he was, whereas, in reality, it seemed to me, he was by nature the opposite of a performer. But a man has a right to perform, and sometimes even an obligation to do so, as I expect he felt he had. He believed he needed to make himself into a kind of easily understood public character, in order to attract attention to his work, which of course deserved all the attention it could possibly get. He was really a saint whose religion was intelligence, or, rather, the exercise of it. I was delighted to hear him speak so fondly of his old acquaintance Charlie Chaplin, another great man I have met, but then both of *you* have met him, and probably know him as he really is better than I do, since both of you have enjoyed prolonged visits in his home, with his kids."

"I have never seen any of his movies," my daughter said. "Not one."

"I saw *Modern Times* last year," my son said, "and frankly I was disappointed. I suppose I had heard so much about his movies, I had expected too much. *Modern Times* is pretty funny, but not as funny as all that. Is Chaplin really a great man?"

"Well, you tell me."

"I don't know."

"He's great all right. He is the greatest man of the movies so far, at any rate, and even if somebody comes along who is greater, which isn't very likely, there can never again be anybody like him. He is spoken of as having been the little man, but that really isn't it at all. What he was, was the lonely man, the incurably and inconsolably lonely man. Well, times have changed, and with the times loneliness has also changed, or, rather, the usage in art of loneliness has changed. It isn't that loneliness is a thing of the past. It isn't. But there is now a good chance that in time loneliness shall become, if not impossible, at least a recognizable form of readily healable illness. How? By means of understanding, of course, by means of intelligence, by means of a decision about loneliness followed by a curative order of attitude and behavior. Essentially, man will always remain lonely, or capable of loneliness, for the reason that each man *is* limited to himself, isolate in body, and even in spirit hardly ever even slightly related to others, excepting in a manner that is inevitably full of all kinds of inaccuracies. Chaplin himself, in his later movies, has sought to abandon the role of the lonely man, and if he hasn't entirely succeeded, he has come near it, and he has tried not to stay in the same place. In another world, in the earlier world, the world of my boyhood, for instance, and the world of the first twenty or thirty years of this century, it was possible for all of us to laugh and cry about our loneliness, as revealed by Chaplin, but this isn't possible any longer. Loneliness, as a device for the achievement of art, in other words, isn't any longer valid —certainly not exclusively. We have got to find out how to make art out of intelligence, too, and I mean popular art, which of course is what Chaplin's art has always been."

"Well," my daughter said, "when he's at home he's always being funny, or trying to be, and I don't want to be disrespectful or anything like that, but it really gets to be boring, and an awful strain. Is it necessary to be funny?"

"In art, it's hardly ever undesirable, and in any case there isn't ever enough of it to permit us to worry about it. In a sense, nothing and nobody *isn't* funny, but we have a habit of not noticing this. It's something like sleight of hand: our attention has been drawn to another aspect of the matter, but if you ever want to find the comic element in anything, if only for the exercise of it, the spiritual calisthenics of it, all you have got to do is keep your eye on the size of the thing, which is always astonishingly small, and bring this size to bear upon the intensity, earnestness, righteousness, and general confusion of the action of the thing. The smallness of the thing itself in relation to the enormity it presumes to be in action constitutes the comic, and will be the fun of it, if you want it to be that way, and you may very well decide you don't."

"O.K.," my son said, "Mr. Huff, Shaw, and Chaplin. Who else?"

"When I think of the great men who were alive and abroad in the world that I didn't meet before they died, and the ones who are still alive, but dying, that I shall never meet, and the new ones coming along all the time, while I myself move nearer to dying, I am annoyed and depressed by my failure—no, my *refusal*—to seek them out, if only to say to each of them in greeting, 'Well, now. What's the matter with *you?*' "

"Well, why in the world would you want to say *that?*"

"To break the ice, of course, so that if anybody has anything to say, he'll say it."

My son said, "But you've never actually said any such thing to anybody at all, let alone to anybody great, and you know it. You are sometimes really very courteous, you know, even more courteous than you really ought to be, and more than most other people are."

"I've said it to a lot of people, but of course I've known them, and they've known me, and so it hasn't been discourteous, it has been impersonal, not about us specifically, but about the failure of light itself, intelligence itself, to find something worth falling upon, something worth illuminating."

"I don't get it."

"No doubt, since I've said it poorly. We don't live long, and by the time we know anything at all, or a way to begin to find out, or at any rate to hope to begin to find out, we are moving lickety-split, as if on skis, down the steep snow slope, passing others also on their way down, and coming face to face with others on their way up, and there just isn't time enough to really meet and talk. About the most we can do is shout something or other in passing, and this circumstance impels me to shout something that isn't entirely silly and useless. Why should I ask a dying man, 'Well, now, how are you?' Why shouldn't I do him a favor and ask him why he's so stupid?"

"Some favor."

"The best, most likely. It might make him *laugh* at any rate."

My kids laughed, and then we agreed to play another game of freeze-out stud.

CHAPTER TWENTY-THREE

In sleep last night I moved to a house in the country, in the snow of winter, and I went to the room where I was to sleep, only to find that the room had become a bird sanctuary: all kinds of birds, two by two, and sometimes four by four and six by six, had found places along the top of the four walls to wait out the winter, half-asleep but warm and safe and together. The place appropriated by the hummingbirds was especially pleasing to me, for I have always loved the little things, and there they were

219

brighter than I had ever seen them in the summertime:
red, green, yellow, and black. The other birds seemed
more than half-asleep; they seemed drugged, and a few of
them seemed almost half-dead, from something or other.
But the hummingbirds were radiantly alive, and there
wasn't any light of the sun anywhere, everything was
gray, except where the hummingbirds were, for they made
their own light.

"Look at those little beauties, will you? Nothing can
stop them, that's all."

And then a dozen different kinds of other birds began
to come out from behind the wall, from the place where
they had taken sanctuary for the winter, and they seemed
to be birds I had actually seen at one time or another, but
apparently mainly in cages in stores where birds are sold,
and there were too many of them.

"Hell, this place is for the birds, it's not for me."

Still, there was nowhere else to go, so I stayed. The
birds came out to behold the intruder, to be frightened
by him, to flutter out of the room into the cold for a
moment, to flutter back, and to find him still there. I
don't remember if I left that place, left it to the birds out
of courtesy or a sense of rightness, since they had been
there first, or if I stayed because there was nowhere else
to go.

Well, now, we do sleep, don't we? And we do live in
our sleep, and sometimes remember a little of it, don't
we? Only a few nights ago I heard my daughter ask my
son what he would rather be than a human being, and

my son said, "A bird, a hawk, I guess, or one of the birds of the sea, a gull maybe."

And we talk, don't we? We ask questions and we answer them, don't we?

My daughter couldn't decide what she would rather be, so she asked what I would rather be. I thought for a moment, and wanted to say a rock, but I knew she wouldn't care for that very much, and in fact it wasn't enough for me, either, even in the little game, so I didn't say a rock, I thought some more: well, what about a bear? But that wasn't it, either. A black panther, perhaps. No, that wasn't it, either. But in the end I said something. I didn't want to spoil the game, but I'll be damned if I can remember what I said, and this *happened*, it wasn't dreamed, it was part of the other reality, the more readily remembered reality, so what was it that I said? Everything is a part of man, of course—every animal, every plant, every large thing, every small thing, every visible and known thing, and every invisible and unknown thing, so that no matter what you say, no matter what you believe or pretend you would rather be, it is already a part of what you are in any case, only less, so how can you even think of preferring to be this other thing? And yet kids are forever asking one another, and the older people they know, such questions. Why do they ask them? And what was my reply? Why can't I remember it? Or didn't I actually make a reply?

In the story about the young man and the tiger there was a question and an answer that pleased and surprised

221

me. The question was ordinary enough, and so it didn't surprise me, although I was pleased that I had written it, because a writer at work has got to write something and anything is better than nothing, but the answer *wasn't* ordinary, even for me, even for that work, which from the beginning had been at least out there where the wild stuff is. The question was asked by a man of seventy who owned a coffee-importing house in New York in 1928. Here was this new worker, Thomas Tracy, making trouble, asking for a promotion after only a few days, while the rest of his workers were satisfied to work and wait for years: here was this upstart from California who wanted to become a coffee-taster, a job reserved for men who had been in the company for twenty years or more. The old man was astonished and annoyed. He said to the California upstart: "What is your work?" Well, the young man's work was to lift and carry the heavy sacks containing coffee beans, the humblest work in the whole establishment, but the boy from California replied, "I write songs." I was delighted by this reply, even though I myself had written it, even though I myself had started the whole thing, had invented, or at any rate had hit upon, the whole complex, the whole way and style of all that was there, and all that was to become there. The answer astonished and annoyed the old man, who nevertheless couldn't help admiring the young man, couldn't help being glad that such a fellow had found his way into his company, a writer of songs. Again, though, that's it, that's all there is to it, there isn't any point, there isn't any connection, unless of course I just don't happen to know there *is* a connection, from ignorance, which isn't entirely unlikely. I am only at work, sick in the head, both from a lingering cold I have tried to ignore, and have ignored, and from a kind of sanity I have cultivated over the years, which while not much better than my usual and natural madness is at least better than nothing, and therefore slightly useful. Hell, there is no plot, there is no story, nothing moves in a nice straight line, everything's all over the place, but most of all the writer won't step aside for longer than an instant and let somebody else take the stage. He is always sticking his big nose into everything. He's *got* the nose to do it with, too. And he does it all the time. Ah, but aren't there books and books? What's the difference if one of them isn't the way the best of the others are, just so it also isn't the way the worst of the others are, either? Well, let me tell you something, old friend, this is this book, that's all, and I am writing it, and I shall finish it, nothing in the world has stopped that, nothing has been able to stop it, and nothing is going to stop it, nothing will ever stop it, because it isn't the book that matters, it's the writer.

What can you expect from a homeless man in a far-away city, a father in a foreign country, a vineyard-worker in a great city?

My son says, "Ptui."

"I've heard you say that six or seven times. What is it? What does it mean?"

"It means ptui, that's all. Nothing."

223

"It doesn't sound as if it means nothing."

"I suppose nothing *sounds* as if it means nothing, but hardly anything really does. What's your book about? Paris?"

"I don't know anything about Paris."

"You're here, though, and this *is* Paris."

"I love Paris," my daughter says, "but I wish we could go to the seashore for a while. When we were in Athens two summers ago we went to the beach at Glyfada every day. I'll never forget the beach at Glyfada, and all those perfect little pebbles there."

"I have the ones you gathered. They're in storage in California, along with all of my manuscripts and other junk."

"You kept the pebbles?"

"Every one of them."

"What in the world for?"

"What did you gather them for? To have, of course. And to look at, or at any rate to be *able* to look at any time you might remember them and *want* to look at them. I wish I could look at them right now."

"To tell you the truth, I do, too," my daughter said. "They were the best pebbles I ever gathered, much better than the ones I gathered on the beach at Malibu. How come the pebbles at Glyfada are all so smooth and color-ful and good to see?"

"Greece is the home of a great culture. It's only right that the pebbles of Greece should reveal that."

"What's the book about?" my son says again.

"It's no good. I'm going to finish it, though."

"A whole month of hard work for nothing?"

"Why for nothing? I've got to *try*, don't I? That's worth something, isn't it? I've got to be willing to fail, don't I? *Again,* I mean. And being willing is worth something, isn't it? I mean, suppose I stopped being willing? I'd have quit, wouldn't I? And what's the good of that?"

"Is it really no good, or are you just saying that, out of superstition or something? I know a lot of writers are superstitious about talking about something they are writing while they're writing it. They think talking about it will spoil it or something. You don't really mean it's no good, do you?"

"I suppose I hope I'm mistaken, at that. But I'm afraid I'm not entirely mistaken this time. I seem to be trying for something, but it really doesn't seem to be working."

"How come? You've had a lot of experience at writing. You know how it's done, and best of all you don't take forever, the way some writers do. How come this book isn't working?"

"Bad luck, I guess."

"Has luck got that much to do with writing? Isn't it a matter of working?"

"Oh, if you work, you'll get a book written, but you have got to have a little luck for the thing to turn out to be something more than just another book. I just can't be pleased about the way this one is turning out."

"How's your head?"

"Not so good. But it's been worse even when I *haven't*

225

been writing a new book, so I can't be bothered about that."

"But you *are* bothered."

"I've been *more* bothered. Not writing, not working at all, trying only to have a pleasant time, my head has been bad and I have been more bothered by it than I am now."

"You can't win?"

"Most likely, but you can at least try not to lose so steadily, because that gets to be damned boring."

"I get a headache, I take a couple of aspirins."

"It's not an ache, it's the head itself, *my* head. Aspirin isn't going to do it any good."

"What is?"

"Water," my daughter said. "The sea. The shore. Where the pebbles are. The minute the book is finished, let's go to the seashore, let's walk into the water, let's sit on the sand, let's gather pebbles, let's do the way we did two summers ago in Athens."

"O.K. There are only a few more days to go, anyway. We'll go to the sea somewhere, or would you rather go to Moscow?"

"Why Moscow?"

My son said, "Would you *really* like to go to Moscow?"

"I wouldn't mind. We'd go by train, to see more of the countryside."

"No," my daughter said, "the hell with Moscow. Let's go to the seashore."

226

"Just a minute," my son said. "We can always go to the seashore."

"We can always go to Moscow, too," my daughter said.

"Well, we'll think about it."

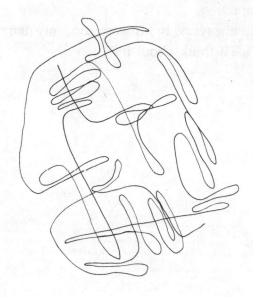

CHAPTER TWENTY-FOUR

I was pruning vines on a vineyard in the San Joaquin Valley of California when I was sixteen years old, after I had been kicked out of school so many times I decided not to go back. Heavy rain began to fall and all of the workers had to quit work for the rest of that day. I went to a bookstore in Fresno, to the back room where the old books were, and I began to look around for something priceless that I could buy for a nickel or a dime. I found a stack of old magazines, but *good* old magazines, not junk magazines, and the name of one of them was the

Dial, which I had heard about. There was only one copy of the *Dial* in the whole store. I asked the old man and he said it was the only copy he had, the only copy he had ever had, he had had it for a year, he didn't even remember how he'd got it. I paid him a dime and I rode my bike home in the heavy rain, the magazine inside my shirt. I read the magazine from cover to cover because it was raining anyway, there was nowhere to go, I couldn't be bothered about going to a movie, there was nothing to do, I had quit school forever, I was going to be a writer or nothing at all, I didn't know how I was going to be a writer, or how (if need be) I was going to be nothing at all, so I sat at the round table on the screen porch and started to read. Christ, what stuff. How did they do it? How did they write that way? Every word just right, every word clearly printed on heavy white paper, every word full of meaning, all of the words together making one short story after another, or one poem after another, or one essay after another, and there I was sixteen and stupid, a lousy reader instead of a great writer. Even so, being a reader was better than nothing, especially if the stuff you were reading was good, as it was, although I knew it was writing I could never do. Those guys knew how, and I didn't. And I probably never would find out how. I would have to learn how to write in a way that would compel editors and publishers to publish my stuff in spite of the fact that I didn't know how to write. And I didn't believe this was impossible, although I also didn't believe it was inevitable. I wasn't sure. No writer at sixteen is. I knew I couldn't write as these writers were writing, though, because I could see they had been to school. In order to write as they were writing I would have to become like them, and how could I do that? It was out of the question. I didn't know them, except one or two by name, but I could almost see them, and it seemed to me they looked like writers, and I knew I didn't look like a writer. They had learning, and I didn't. I had wisdom, though, or at any rate I believed I did, or else how was I to account for the arrogance I had for everything and everybody in the whole world, including these writers, whose writing on the one hand I admired, whose learning on the other I resented? They had picked up a lot of information about other writers, other periods of writing, and all kinds of theories about what this particular writer had done, how he had in fact started a whole new school of writing, as they said, and all sorts of other things like that. And what did I know about stuff like that? Almost nothing, although I knew the *last words* of two or three hundred men, as reported in an old almanac, one of my favorite books. Before I reached the end of the magazine, though, I came upon four or five pages of writing that made me jump for joy. The stuff had been lifted out of a large, unfinished work entitled *The Oral History of the World,* and the name of the writer was Joe Gould. Well, now, when a writer calls himself Joe instead of Joseph, you stop and wonder. Whose little old pal is *he* trying to be? Before I began to read what Joe Gould had written, I figured him for a phony, and I came near skipping what he had written. I found that I couldn't skip it, though. I read it and jumped, because this was plain, this was straight, this was the real thing, and all it was, was people talking. And they weren't great people saying great things, they were ordinary people saying ordinary things.

I went back to the vineyard the next morning and I began to listen to the ordinary things the other workers said to one another, and to me, and there it was: I had something, Joe Gould had put me wise to something: listen and you shall hear. And I listened.

We talk, we talk all the time, and when we write we don't stop talking, we go right on, it is all talk. I kept looking around for more stuff by Joe Gould, but there just wasn't any more of it. I kept waiting for the book to be published, to arrive at the Public Library, so that I could read the whole thing, because I didn't buy books in those days, except a dictionary, and I did that only once, because once is enough. But the book didn't come out. I kept remembering Joe Gould and his big book, and I went right on looking forward to the happy day when I would see it, and read it from cover to cover, which I knew I would do, because there just wasn't any such thing as getting too much of that kind of writing. The years went by, but still there was no book by Joe Gould in the world. Well, where the hell was the man? What had happened to him? Had he died, or what? Where was his book? Another year went by, and then another, but still no book, and now I myself had published two books, and a third was about to be published.

I was in New York, and I knew Joe Gould was in New York, too, if he was anywhere at all. But I've got it all wrong, so I've got to go back and get it right.

What actually happened was that I read the fragment from his book in the *Dial* and went back to work the next morning, and one day when I was in New York, thirteen or fourteen years later—wrong again.

One of the greatest men in this whole world, who made drawings of plays in rehearsal for the New York *Times* and for the *Herald Tribune,* a man who loved New York and made drawings of the windy streets and the hurrying people in them, moving in and with the wind, a man named Don Freeman, came along one day in New York and opened his sketchbook and showed me the drawings he had made that day. They were great, and I said I wished I had a book for him to illustrate. A year or so later I had such a book and he illustrated it, and he wrote to me in San Francisco from New York. He sent me a magazine he himself got out every now and then called *Newsstand,* full of his drawings. In one of them was a drawing of a full-bearded man with twinkling eyes, and the name of this man was Joe Gould. The minute I got back to New York I telephoned Don Freeman and asked him if he could tell me something about Joe Gould.

"Hell," he said, "I'll take you to him, or bring him to you."

Well, Joe Gould was a little bit of a fellow with a kind of birdlike voice. I told him how I had found his piece in the *Dial,* and had never been able to forget it, where was

232

the whole book? He said he was still writing it. Well, why not publish parts of it in the magazines? Well, he didn't know. Well, how much of it had he written so far? Well, a million words of it. Well, that's the equivalent of four or five novels—long ones, not short ones. Why not publish the book in three or four, or even five or six volumes? Why wait any longer? Well, he didn't know. For one thing, he didn't know where most of the manuscript was. He hadn't quite lost it, although he may have. He had forgotten it in one or another of the many rooming houses in New York where he had lived for a while. Well, did he have *some* of the manuscript? Yes, he had quite a lot of it. Well, did he want to publish what he had? Well, maybe. He hadn't looked at the stuff, he was busy writing new stuff. Well, did he have any of the new stuff. Yes, he had some of it in his back pocket. He brought some stuff out of his back pocket, six or seven kinds of paper, folded together, on which he had written more of the book, and he read a couple of pages of the stuff, and it was great. What you read at sixteen may not mean very much to you when you're twenty-eight or twenty-nine, but Joe Gould's new stuff was just as good as his old stuff, if in fact it wasn't better, as I believe it was. Well, it's no good having stuff like that all over the place, some of it lost, all of it likely to become lost, since Joe Gould had no permanent address, had no money, lived from one day to the next, a man in his middle fifties at that time. Stuff like that ought to be published, so that others might know about it, read it, have it, so that I, for instance, might. So how about it? Well, everybody *knew* he was writing the book, Joe said. Everybody in the publishing world knew he had been writing it for twenty years or more, but nobody had invited him to offer the stuff for publication. Well, this was just plain silly, so I had to say, "Now, Joe, please tell me, is it possible you *prefer* not to have this book published, for some reason?" Joe said he didn't prefer not to have the stuff published, but at the same time he didn't especially mind that it hadn't been. I had to drink a little more and I had to think a little more about this. Joe had become a kind of legend, to begin with. He was famous in the little saloons of Greenwich Village. He had a lot of friends, most of them writers and painters, and most of them without money, too, although none of them were so steadily and consistently without it. Also, was it possible that he had in reality written very little during the years since the *Dial* had published a little of his writing, and he was only pretending that he had written a lot, had lost a lot, had misplaced a lot? What was the truth? He had certainly produced some of the work, brought it out of his back pocket, and from the looks of it, the writing was new, it had been done earlier that day, or yesterday, or the day before, he seemed to be at work on the book all the time, the talk was about new stuff in the world, very recent stuff, the big names discussed by the talkers were new big names, so what was going on? It seemed to me that while I did not want to intrude, I owed it to writing itself, and I owed it to myself, if not to Joe himself, to do something about having some of his great work published.

Joe said, "O.K., but I don't think any publisher will be willing to publish any of the stuff."

I wanted to know why not, and he said, "Well, *you* like it, and I *believe* in it, and Don likes it, and a lot of other people I have read some of it to like it, but it isn't the kind of stuff publishers like, the kind of stuff they are used to, the kind they believe will make a lot of money, but go ahead if you want to."

I visited my publisher and we talked about it and he said he would be very happy to see the stuff if Joe would take it up to his office. I told Joe, and I believed he would actually go up there with some of the manuscript, but at the same time I couldn't help noticing that he wasn't excited about the idea, and again I felt I just didn't understand what was going on. In the end, over a period of six or seven years, I spoke first to Joe about the book and then to a publisher, a new one each time, six or seven of them, and I always believed, or hoped, Joe would take some of his manuscript to one of the publishers and the publisher would bring it out in the form of a book, under Joe's title for it, *The Oral History of the World*. But it didn't happen, and Joe died.

At first Joe disappeared, or at any rate nobody saw him around, although one or two must have known what had happened to him. I heard about it later: Joe had spent the last three years of his life in a kind of lunatic asylum, but you have got to bear in mind that if Joe needed a place where he could rest a little at last it would more than likely be his preference to go to a place reserved for

235

people who are so alive as to seem mad. He was close to seventy by then, and he had been homeless for the better part of his life, one of the most erudite men in the world, a member of a famed family which he had long since forsaken, which in turn had long since forsaken him, a character in the Village, a laughing little fellow whose false teeth now and then fell out of his mouth, and were once stepped upon and crushed accidentally, who smoked incessantly, placing his cigarettes into a long holder from Woolworth's, whose gray beard was stained brown all around his mouth, who lived in his clothes, who was dirty and dynamic all his life.

A rich New Yorker once asked me if I might be able to get Joe to take a bath and put on new clothes supplied by the New Yorker and then go to dinner at the New Yorker's house. I said no. And nothing more. I was willing to try to get Joe interested in the idea of having his great book published, but I'd be damned if I would ask him to become a bathed and neatly dressed freak for the amusement of a millionaire.

But we talk, don't we? We talk all the time, and Joe Gould was the only man in the world who hit upon the idea that our history and our meaning might be best revealed *through* our talk. But the book was never published. We don't have it. The manuscript was written and lost, or it wasn't written. Or it was written, and ignored. Certainly nobody in our world was able to get Joe Gould either to show what he had written or to settle down and start writing what he had said he had written, whichever is nearest the truth. Nobody, including myself.

CHAPTER TWENTY-FIVE

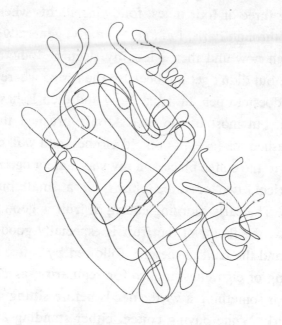

I have done it, for which I thank God. I thank my father, my mother, their fathers and mothers. I thank Columbus, Galileo, Marco Polo, Greeks, Italians, Egyptians, Moors, Spaniards, Jews, Germans, Russians, Persians, the French, the English, the Chinese, the Japanese, and all of the other named peoples, especially the Kurds and the Basques. And I thank my son and my daughter.

Now, I will tell you how I did it, in case you want to do it, too.

First, I tried to get up early every morning, and excepting three or four times, following nights when I had roared through Paris, I *did* get up early, generally at five, although now and then I left my sleep at four, or even earlier, but didn't get up, because the *bistro* where I take coffee doesn't open until six. Now and then I shaved and bathed, but most of the time I only brushed the teeth and washed the face, put on old clothes, and walked three blocks to the coffee place. On my way I ate a fig, a peach, an apricot, two or three plums, or a small bunch of grapes. The early-morning eating of fruit is good for two reasons: the flavor of the fruit is especially good at that hour, and the fruit in the gut, followed by coffee and the smoking of cigarettes, makes for regularity, as they say, which is something a writer needs before sitting down to his work. While having coffee, either standing at a bar, or sitting at a small sidewalk table, I glanced at the Paris *Herald Tribune,* and I studied the results of the previous day's horse races in a newspaper called *Paris-Turf.* About an hour after I had gotten out of bed I sat down at my worktable and I began to write. I asked of myself at least six pages of new writing every day, but after a while, as I had expected, it came to pass that I wrote more pages at each sitting, until finally I found that I was writing nine pages. Twice I wrote extra chapters, going to work in the evening because my kids had gone to the movies, and I believed it would be interesting to see if I might manage something while they were gone. One of these extra chapters was a kind of letter to God. I have forgotten what the other was.

Every morning after I had done my work, I clipped the pages together and placed them in a folder. At the end of every seven days I gathered together the seven chapters, counted the number of pages, and removed them from the folder. There were forty-five pages in the first seven days of work, forty-seven in the second, fifty-nine in the third, sixty-nine in the fourth, and there are likely to be thirty-seven in the last three days of work, making a total of around two hundred and fifty pages, give or take six or seven pages either way. Each of these pages has about fifty lines of writing, and each line has about ten or eleven words, making a total of about five hundred words per page, as the saying is. If this is so, the book will be a book of about a hundred and twenty-five thousand words, which isn't much, but also isn't little. I like revising a book, it is as much a part of writing as writing itself is: it is in fact the most important part of it, and I have every intention of revising this book some day. In case I don't, let it be understood that I intended to, that I am not unaware of having permitted all manner of flaws to stand, as I wrote, feeling I would prefer to remove them at a later time, when I would be in a position to consider the book as a whole thing. I have frequently fallen into a style of writing that I know must prove annoying to the reader in that phrases are repeated, for clarity of course, all the while knowing that I might not need so much clarity, especially if the clarity made for monotony, which I am sure it frequently did. It was necessary to smoke about a package of cigarettes in the writing of a new chapter.

After work I met with my kids, to discuss the day's activities. I kept after them to keep after themselves, to make drawings, to make water-color paintings, to write, to read, to look carefully at all things, to think clearly, to visit art galleries, to walk, to have fun. Now and then the three of us took off together, for the adventure of being abroad in the streets of Paris, with money enough in our pockets to buy anything we might care to buy: food, drink, clothing, shoes, books, magazines, admission to theaters, and so on and so forth. My son bought a fine drawing by Picasso for a hundred and fifty dollars, his own money, saved up all his life, as he put it. It is a drawing of a bird, a peace bird, as he described it in his report to his mother, which he wanted to read to me. For about a hundred dollars he bought a drawing of a head, Greek-like, so to say, by Matisse. Both of the drawings are framed in glass, and priceless. His fortune has now been reduced to sixty-five thousand francs, or about a hundred and thirty dollars. I have handed each of them at least ten thousand francs a week to spend as they please, and they have bought stuff by which to make pictures, all of which I have found exciting and excellent, and have kept for them. I have insisted that each of them sign and date each of his drawings, as I know the drawings will be of great interest to them later on, perhaps much later on. We have had some fights, some small ones,

240

some big ones, and a couple of very big ones. The biggest
were with my son, of course, who is fighting his life, as my
family puts it: this is a necessary fight for a growing
boy, as I have told him, as he is beginning to understand.
One day, to illustrate what I mean, he remarked that
when he was seven or eight or nine, or possibly even
when he was ten or eleven, he frequently thought, This
man, and this woman, they *aren't* my father and my
mother, they just *can't* be.

Two or three times my daughter became a *grande dame,*
a prima donna, who simply couldn't tolerate her ignorant,
inferior, impossible, uncouth, and unfair father.

Now and then I became an idiot, believing my kids
were worthless, on account of their mother: it was not my
fault, not the fault of my family, not the fault of my class,
the working, proud, intelligent, creative, healthy, and
comic poor, who of course remain in this class no matter
how much money they make or have. In the end, though,
I loved them, including their flaws, or even *for* their
flaws, and they perhaps in turn loved me.

A dozen times or more my son and I took a taxi to
one or another of the Paris race tracks. Several times
when we saw our choice coming down to the wire ahead
of the field we faced one another and shook hands. We
lost, too, and noticed how it affected us, what a fool
losing made of each of us, at least for a moment. Three
times we picked the right horse in the last race of the day
and bet all the money we had, and thereby broke even, or
won a little. I enjoyed going to the races, because I like

241

getting out to the country, I like forgetting my work, and I like to puzzle over the outcome of a horse race, to see if I can guess what the outcome is going to be, and to watch the fulfillment or frustration of my guess. I took sick with something I have agreed to call a virus of some kind, and I am still there, still sick, although no longer fiercely.

My kids took sick with the same thing, and only last night my daughter, setting the table for the supper she and I had prepared, said, "We have all got a touch of virus, or a touch of the poet, or something."

I said, "By the time you get up tomorrow morning it will be written, the book will be finished."

"Can you just stop anywhere?"

"Well, not quite, although this is the kind of book that you *can,* almost—anything will do, although I have from the beginning tried to write the thing in such a way that it might perhaps turn out to have had some kind of form, after all."

"But isn't it possible you might find at the last minute that you must write another day, or two or three, more?"

"No, this book is going to be finished tomorrow morning, win, lose, or draw."

She was pleased about that, because if I am not writing a book, if I am not at work, we can think about going somewhere, for instance.

This afternoon I shall discuss with my kids where we shall go, and how we shall go. I have the red racer in the garage of the George V Hotel. It was the buying of this car in Belgrade from the First Assistant to the Mexican Ambassador to Yugoslavia almost five months ago that has brought me to this moment, or, rather, to the unexpected events of the past five months, which were not planned.

Had I not bought the car it might very well be that I would not have written the play I wrote in May, or this book, for the car took me entirely away from the plans I had made in New York in February. It took me to freedom, although it was a dangerous freedom, in that I found it first desirable to gamble and then necessary to do so. The gambling, drinking, roaring, and losing accelerated the dying that has always been in me, and on one occasion it almost threw me out. I dreamed in a suffocating terror that my brother had come instantly from more than half across the world, not in spirit alone, but in body as well, to ask if I had died. And for a moment I wasn't sure I hadn't. I wasn't sure my brother's question was not in fact my death. I wasn't sure that this was not the way a man died, the way I *had* died, in suffocating sleep. Somebody in your family who has known you from the first day of life comes to you swiftly, fiercely, with love that is all the more love in that it is angry, your own blood angry at you for failure, and demands of you an explanation for the grief your failure is causing, trying all the while to smile, to believe he has not been too late, that you may be able to reply that you have *not* died. Nothing of that kind had ever before happened to me. I woke up and wondered.

In Paris, where I really didn't want to be, I took to the town on its own terms, as they are stated in the streets. The little money I had salvaged carried me along, but something would have to be done soon, and I didn't like the idea of facing up to that at all. I therefore bought lottery tickets, hoping I might win fifty million francs, collect my money, and tell nobody about it: just turn around and drive to Valencia. I *had* one winning ticket, as a matter of fact—for a net profit of fifty cents.

I went to work and wrote a play for money.

I didn't die.

I brought my kids to my own home, even if it is a temporary one, and in a few minutes we are going to discuss where to go and what to do for the rest of the summer.

I never did find out what happened to the young man from the *Paris Review* who borrowed a tape-recorder.